Alesha Dixon first found fame as part of
BRIT-nominated and MOBO Award-winning
group Mis-Teeq, which achieved 2 platinum albums
and 7 top ten hits, before going on to become
a platinum-selling solo artist in her own right.
Alesha's appearance on *Strictly Come Dancing*
in 2007 led to her winning the series and
becoming a judge for three seasons.

Since then she has presented and hosted many TV
shows including CBBC dance show *Alesha's Street
Dance Stars, Children In Need, Comic Relief,* BBC1's *The
Greatest Dancer, America's Got Talent: The Champions,
Australia's Got Talent* and for a decade has been a hugely
popular judge on *Britain's Got Talent.*

ALSO AVAILABLE

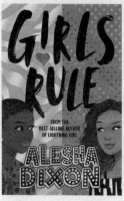

LUNA WOLF

CODE: DANGER

ALESHA DIXON

ILLUSTRATED BY DEISE LINO

SCHOLASTIC

Published in the UK by Scholastic, 2024
1 London Bridge, London, SE1 9BG
Scholastic Ireland, 89E Lagan Road, Dublin Industrial Estate, Glasnevin,
Dublin, D11 HP5F

ISBN 978 0702 32411 6

A CIP catalogue record for this book is available from the British Library.

Printed and bound in Great Britain by Clays Ltd, Elcograf S.p.A
Paper made from wood grown in sustainable forests and other controlled
sources.

1 3 5 7 9 10 8 6 4 2

www.scholastic.co.uk

I dedicate this book to
my mother, Beverley.

Her deep love, affection and
dedication towards the freedom
and respect of animals is
unwavering.

CHAPTER ONE

Feeling the warmth of the sun on my face, I lie back on the picnic blanket and close my eyes. My hand is resting on the soft fur of my dog, Silver, who is sitting next to me, his eyes fixed on a squirrel running along the branch of a tree in next door's garden.

"Relax, Silver," I say without opening my eyes, giving him a pat. "We only have one more week of the summer holidays together. You'll have all day to patrol the garden for squirrels when I'm at school. Don't you want to enjoy the time we have left?"

He lets out a small whine in reply and I smile to myself.

"Leave the squirrel alone," I press.

Relenting, he shakes his head and moves to curl up next to me with a heavy sigh.

"I know, I know," I say, giving him a tickle behind the ears. "I wish you could come to school with me too, but no dogs allowed. Imagine what they'd say if they knew that you weren't just any dog and could transform into a wolf. If dogs aren't allowed, it's unlikely that wolves would be."

He huffs, burying his nose under my arm.

"I agree, it is a silly rule," I say, chuckling.

I know it might seem strange to have full-blown conversations with a dog, but ever since I adopted Silver from the local rescue centre, I've felt that he's been able to understand me – even before I knew we had a magical connection.

As he nestles closer, enjoying a peaceful moment bathing in the sunshine, my free hand instinctively flies to the pendant hanging around my neck to check that it's still there. I never take it off. It used to belong to my mum and now it belongs to me.

2

So does its magic.

I always knew that Mum was an amazing, successful scientist who, before she died, dedicated her life to developing medicines for animals, but until the events of this summer, I had no idea that she'd been the leading scientist on a project named Magnitude. Using the incredible discovery of a magical source that had the ability to enhance animals into super versions of themselves, Magnitude was founded to research the magic so that it could be harnessed to protect and help animals in need.

Or so Mum thought.

But it turned out that she had been used by the evil boss behind Magnitude. Whoever he was, he had fooled her into thinking that she – the only person who could wield the magic – would be doing it for good. In fact, he and Mum's jealous colleague, Dr Callahan, had plans to create super animals to sell on the black market to international collectors. They didn't care about the animals' welfare.

When Mum discovered their plan, she was

horrified. She ran away with the only five super animals in existence and left them in the care of her loyal friend, journalist Rex Robinson, at his country estate, so that they could be safe. Little did she know that years later, after she'd passed away, Callahan and his cronies would track them down and steal them in the hope of relaunching Magnitude. Thankfully, Silver managed to escape and instinctively went looking for my mum, the only human he could trust, and that's how he ended up at the local rescue centre near my nan. When I arrived there at the beginning of the summer, I didn't choose to adopt him – he chose me.

It was lucky that I had Silver at my side when Callahan tracked me down in the hope of stealing my necklace, the one that Mum had insisted Dad give to me and no one else. Now we know why: its blue pendant is the last of the magical source that transforms the animals. Everyone, including the founder of Magnitude and his employee Callahan, had thought she'd destroyed it all, but she'd kept one last piece. Callahan got his hands on it, but it wouldn't work for him. The magic worked only for my mum and now it works for me.

Talk about BIG responsibility.

Thankfully, we stopped Callahan's evil plans and he and his cronies landed themselves in prison, and we saved the other four super animals: Blizzard, the ferret who transforms into a polar bear; Chomp, a gecko who becomes a crocodile; Stripes the tabby cat, who is secretly a tiger; and Talon, a sparrow who transforms into an eagle. They live here with me, Dad and Silver at Nan's house.

It's the perfect living situation.

CRASH!!

I wince at the loud bang that comes from the kitchen, followed swiftly by the inevitable cry from Nan:

"BLIZZARD! You naughty, naughty ferret!"

Silver lifts his head and gives me a knowing look as I push myself up on my elbows.

"Blizzard has landed us in trouble again, hasn't he," I mutter to him.

Sure enough, I suddenly feel sharp ferret claws digging into my arm as Blizzard, having come zooming out of the kitchen into the garden, scurries up my arm and curls round my neck, taking refuge there. The commotion has caused Stripes to hop down from the top of the garden shed where she was happily sunbathing and come slinking across the lawn towards us, followed by Chomp the gecko, who was taking a dip in the birdbath. He crawls up on to my ankle.

"Luna Wolf!"

I grimace at the sharp tone in Nan's voice as she bellows my full name and comes storming out of the kitchen wearing bright pink leggings and a neon-orange gym top with a thunderous expression on her face. Given the fact that I have no doubt I'm about to be told off, I try not to laugh at the fact that Talon is perched atop Nan's head.

Nan claims that she loves all the animals equally, but she has a hard time hiding how much she favours the company of the mighty little sparrow. We often hear Nan nattering away to Talon, telling her all about the family dramas or spouting her opinions on the news and current events. She likes to complain about the other animals to the lofty and superior Talon, who also finds their chaotic tendencies tiresome.

"Hey, Nan," I say brightly, in the hope of lifting the mood. "What's up?"

"*What's up?*" she repeats, her eye twitching in anger. "WHAT'S UP?"

Uh-oh.

"What is *up*, Luna, is that your ferret has yet again successfully knocked over the salt-fish fritters that I spent HOURS cooking this morning," Nan seethes, shaking her finger at Blizzard. "I had made them specially to bring to my aerial yoga class this afternoon! Gerard was particularly excited to taste them. Now they're splattered all over my kitchen floor!"

I blink at her. "Who's Gerard?"

Her expression softens. "He's … he's a friend. A fellow aerial yoga devotee." She hesitates, shaking her head and frowning again. "Never you mind

7

who Gerard is! The point is, my salt-fish fritters are completely ruined and it's all because of your mischievous ferret and his tendency to use my kitchen as his own personal jungle gym."

"I'm sorry, Nan, I'll have a word with him."

She folds her arms. "Just like yesterday when you had a word with him after he knocked over the vase in the lounge?"

"Uh…"

"And the day before that when he was using the sofa as a trampoline?"

"Well—"

"And the day before that when I discovered him in the fridge, having consumed the majority of its contents?"

"In Blizzard's defence, you were the one who shut him in the fridge in the first place."

She narrows her eyes at me. I know I've made a grave mistake.

"I shouldn't have to check my fridge for rogue ferrets before shutting the door, Luna," she hisses. "Now, I know I said I was happy to provide a temporary home for these animals while you and your dad look for a new house, but it's getting out of control!"

"I'm sorry, Nan, but it's difficult for Blizzard! He gets bored easily and has to look for new ways to entertain himself. Remember, he's part polar bear. He's special."

She sighs impatiently. "Then maybe these special animals don't belong here."

"Of course they do! They belong wherever I am. We're connected."

"I know, and I appreciate that it's a wonderful connection you have with these animals, but you'd have that no matter where you all are. Remember, your mum had the same connection and she didn't live in the same house as them," Nan points out.

"That's because they were cooped up in a laboratory," I grumble. "Nan, you're not seriously considering kicking them out, are you?"

She raises her eyes to the sky. "No, not today. But" – she waggles her finger again in Blizzard's direction – "if that ferret knocks over one more thing in my house, he'll be in BIG trouble, you understand?"

I nod. "Sorry about the salt–fish fritters. I hope Gerard isn't too disappointed."

"I'll just have to make more for our class next week," she reasons grumpily. "Hopefully the next one won't be sabotaged by a rodent."

"Actually, ferrets aren't rodents," I correct her. "They do look similar, but ferrets are members of the mustelid family."

"Is that so?" She looks at me curiously before allowing a small smile. "You know, sometimes, Luna, you sound just like your mother."

"Really?" I say hopefully.

"Athena would often spout animal facts at me. Just like you, she spent a lot of her free time with her nose in a book about wolves or big cats or..."

She trails off, lost in a memory. A flash of sadness crosses her face, like it always does when she talks about Mum. I reach up to touch my necklace again. Nan notices the gesture and takes a deep breath in.

"I have to go if I'm going to make it to aerial yoga," she announces. "And don't you dare let Blizzard near the trifle that I've left on the kitchen counter – I've made that for Miss Herring, who lives at number twelve. She's coming to pick it up in a couple of minutes to take to her boyfriend's dinner party. He's under the impression that she's an excellent cook."

"I'll keep Blizzard out here where he can't get into any trouble. Promise."

"That ferret is nothing but trouble," Nan mutters, before giving me a wave. "I'll see you when I get back."

"Have fun!" I call after her as she turns to head

inside, crossing paths with my dad, who emerges from the kitchen out into the garden at the same time.

"Ah, Richard, how did the house hunting go?" she asks him.

He shakes his head, defeated. She gives him a comforting pat on the shoulder and then disappears into the house. Dad makes his way across the grass towards me.

"Is Nan aware that there's a bird on her head, do you think?" he asks, crouching down to give Silver a pat on the head.

"Not sure, but Talon will enjoy aerial yoga if she ends up there."

"Nan's off to another of her classes, is she?" he observes, chuckling as Silver gives him a slobbery lick across the cheek. "I don't think I've ever met anyone as active and sociable as your nan. She's always busy doing something or going out somewhere or cooking something for someone."

"Add 'yelling at the ferret' to that list," I inform him gravely.

He raises his eyebrows at Blizzard, who hasn't budged from round my neck, a position which is growing more and more uncomfortable in the sunshine – I wouldn't choose to wear a furry scarf in this weather.

"Oh dear, what did he do this time?" Dad asks, bemused.

"He ruined another of Nan's dishes. I said I'd have a word with him."

"I'm not sure Blizzard pays much attention when you have words with him."

I lift my finger to affectionately tickle Blizzard under the chin. He gives a grateful squeak before rubbing his little nose against my cheek.

"No, I don't think he does, either, but it's hard to stay mad at him," I giggle. "How were all the house viewings today, Dad?"

"Long, tiring and pointless. There is still nothing suitable in Tottenham that's both within our budget and can fit us as well as five animals that have the potential to transform into … well … much bigger animals," he says, looking deflated. "I keep hoping that something will magically become available, but so far I've had no luck."

"Something will come up," I assure him.

"That's what Lucy keeps saying," he says. "Speaking of whom, have you been down to the rescue centre today?"

"It's Saturday. She insisted I have the day off."

Dad chuckles. "I think you'd move into the rescue centre given half the chance."

"Always an option!" I smile.

It's thanks to Dad's girlfriend, Lucy, that Silver and I found each other in the first place. When Dad first announced at the beginning of the summer that he'd been offered a new job in London, so we'd be moving from our house in the middle of the countryside to stay with Nan in Tottenham for a bit, I was stunned, but I was even more shocked to find out that Dad had been secretly dating someone in the city, too.

It took me a while to adjust to the idea of Dad

14

being with anyone who wasn't Mum, but it helped that Lucy loved animals as much as I did and owned the dog and cat rescue centre down the road where Silver was being housed. Dad encouraged me to spend time there during the holidays getting to know her and her son, Kieron, who's my age and volunteers at the rescue centre when he can to help his mum.

It's actually been kind of cool to see my dad so happy again now that he's found Lucy, and Kieron and I have become friends too. When Lucy and Dad got kidnapped by Callahan, who was trying to pressure me to hand over the necklace in exchange for their safe return, it was Kieron who helped me and Silver fight Callahan and his cronies, freeing Dad and Lucy and rescuing all the animals.

If anything is going to bond two families together, it's a kidnap plot.

"I've been meaning to ask, how are you feeling about school?" Dad asks suddenly. "One week left and it's the start of a brand-new term. You excited? Nervous?"

15

"Both," I answer, butterflies flitting around my stomach. "Although, more nervous than excited."

"That's normal," he assures me. "Starting a new year is always going to be daunting."

"It's not just a new year, it's a new school, too. What if I don't fit in? I didn't exactly fit in at my last one," I recall glumly.

"Things will be different here, Luna," Dad says, offering me an encouraging smile. "For a start, you already know you have a friend there. Kieron is in your year."

"Yeah, I suppose."

"If you don't mind me pointing it out, you've also come on leaps and bounds with your confidence. Ever since you discovered your magical powers, it's like you know who you are," he says proudly, stroking Silver's head and glancing over at me. "You've always been special, Luna. These animals have simply shown it to you."

"Thanks, Dad. If only they could come to school with me," I comment, lifting Blizzard from around my neck so I can lie back again, setting him down on the grass. He scampers off in the direction of the house.

Dad follows suit, lying next to me. He squints up at the bright blue sky and smiles as Stripes hops up on to his chest and curls up there.

"Have you, by any chance, spoken to Nan yet about who's going to be looking after the animals while you're at school and I'm at work?" Dad asks curiously, stroking the cat absent-mindedly.

"Not yet," I admit, closing my eyes. "I thought I might leave that conversation to you."

He chuckles. "Nice try, Luna. I'd speak to her sooner rather than later. I'd say she's already assumed that she'll be left in charge, but out of courtesy, you should talk to her about it and make sure she's happy with the arrangement."

"Fine," I sigh. "I'll speak to her later today."

CRASH!!

I open my eyes in horror and Dad sits bolt upright. He winces, glancing in the direction of the kitchen.

Blizzard appears in the doorway covered in custard and whipped cream.

"On second thoughts," I say, burying my face in my hands, "I think I'll leave that chat until tomorrow."

CHAPTER TWO

"Hey! Watch out!"

Kieron jumps out of the way of three teenage boys racing up the path on their bikes as they narrowly miss crashing into him, cycling past in a blur. They pedal off into the distance, cackling with laughter.

Rolling his eyes, Kieron sighs.

"So much for a quiet walk," he remarks.

We've taken the train out of London into the countryside, a fun excursion that has become something of a weekend tradition. Dad and Lucy research beautiful walks and plan the trips, insisting that it's a good idea to give Silver the space for a proper run. I always find it amusing when they say that because whether it's in woodlands, open fields or an enclosed London park, Silver stays stuck to my side at all times.

Still, it is nice to bring the animals to new places to explore and it's easy to see how much they love it. Whenever we set off on a new trail, Talon soars overhead, somersaulting through the air; Blizzard zigzags through the long glass, letting out chirps of excitement – or "dooking" as I learned recently from studying a book on ferrets; and Stripes bounds along the path, pouncing on every insect she can spot. Chomp tends to stay put on my shoulder, although sometimes if I see a nice little rocky area, I'll pop him down on it and encourage him to have a look around.

I have wondered whether I should use the magic to let them transform when we're out on isolated walks where there's no one for miles, but it's too risky – our group is already a bit of a strange sight for people we bump into and we've received plenty of comments about how "interesting" it is to see a cat and a ferret being taken for a walk, and that's when they don't notice the gecko under my collar and the sparrow lingering overhead.

Imagine what people would say if they saw us strolling along with a wolf, polar bear, tiger, eagle and crocodile in tow.

"By the way, I've decided to launch a newspaper," Kieron announces, as we carry on up the path now that it's free of cyclists.

I turn to look at him in surprise. "Really?"

"It hit me last night: our school doesn't have a newspaper! Isn't that strange? I thought I'd work on a pitch over the next few weeks, speak to the head teacher, Ms Sanderson, and with any luck, she'll give me the go-ahead to launch it next term – the perfect start to the New Year. Every community needs a newspaper, don't you think?"

"I guess so."

"And if anyone is going to set up a newspaper at school, it should be me," he states firmly, sliding his black-framed glasses back up his nose. "I'm the only one there with formal journalistic credentials. I'm a shoo-in for the role of editor-in-chief."

I smile to myself. "That's true," I agree.

"I'd have already made it as a famous journalist if you'd let me write an article about everything that's happened to us this summer," he says wistfully. "If I could write about the super animals, Callahan's attempt to capture them and our heroic efforts to free them, I probably would have won a Pulitzer by now. I'd be the youngest-ever recipient of the prize."

"We agreed it would be best to keep the magic a secret from the world," I remind him, glancing at Silver trotting along at my feet. "If people knew what these animals could do—"

"I know, I know. We don't want to attract any unwanted attention in case evil people want to steal them." Kieron sighs. "But I'm just saying, the *one* time something exciting happens in my life I'm not allowed to tell the world about it. Remember how

I took down one of Callahan's men using a dog's tennis-ball blaster? No one will ever know how awesome that was."

I laugh, before he launches into an entertaining and passionate retelling of the incident, even though I was there and witnessed it first-hand. But Kieron is so good at storytelling and I find myself enraptured anyway.

The first time we met, he told me about his ambitions to be a journalist and, since the events of the summer, his determination to achieve his dream has only increased. Rex Robinson, the famous journalist who secretly looked after the animals for years when Mum first rescued them, anonymously contacted Kieron to help with his research on Magnitude when he started doing some digging on them after Callahan broke into the rescue centre in his hunt for Silver. Impressed by Kieron's dedication to uncovering the truth, Rex has stayed in touch while he travels the globe looking for his next story, and has become Kieron's mentor, encouraging him to send him his stories so he can give pointers. We've never met him in person, but hopefully when he returns to the UK, he'll visit.

I have lots of questions to ask him about Mum. Knowing that she chose him to look after the animals and protect them from the powerful people behind Magnitude means a lot. She must have really trusted him.

"So," Kieron begins, nudging me with his elbow, "are you nervous?"

I frown in confusion. "About you launching a newspaper?"

"No, about going to a new school."

"Oh. A little."

"I would be, too," he says, before his cheeks flush. "I mean, I'm not saying that *you* need to be. Because you don't need to be. Nervous, that is. What I'm saying is that if it were me, *I* would also be nervous … but you don't need to be nervous because you'll be fine."

I chuckle. "It's OK, Kieron, I get what you mean."

He runs a hand through his already-dishevelled dark hair. "Phew!"

"I'm glad that we'll be in the same year."

"Me too. Anyway, considering you spent your summer taking down bad guys with a bunch of super animals and your newfound magical powers, I reckon you can handle a new school," he points out.

"That's true, although somehow school seems scarier," I admit quietly.

"You'll be fine, and remember you have your fam—" He stops himself abruptly, stumbling over his words and clearing his throat, before continuing: "Er… You have us if you need."

"Thanks," I say quickly, pretending not to notice his cheeks flushing.

We both know that Dad and Lucy want us to see ourselves as a *family* now, but I guess Kieron is finding it just as hard to get his head round it all as I am.

It's not that I don't like Lucy – I do, and I love that

she makes Dad happy. And I feel really lucky to have a friend like Kieron. But for a long time it was me and Dad, the two of us. There's a lot of things we used to do together that we don't any more — small things, like movie nights or trips to the ice cream shop. Either there's no time to fit them in around looking for a house, my volunteering at the rescue centre or his date nights, or if we do have the chance to do stuff like that, Lucy and Kieron join us. It sounds petty, but as happy as I am to expand our family, I also miss what we had when it was just me and Dad.

Worst of all, when I find myself really enjoying time with Lucy, I get this wave of guilt about forgetting Mum. As though I'm betraying her somehow. No one could ever replace her and I know that Lucy would never expect to — if anything, she encourages Dad and me to talk about Mum more. I guess I'm scared that if we become this big new happy family, we're in danger of forgetting the family we once had. I don't ever want to risk that. I think about Mum all the time and I especially miss her when there's so much change going on.

So I can understand why Kieron tripped over the word "family" when referring to us and our parents. Saying it out loud makes it real, and I'm not sure either of us is prepared to accept that quite yet.

As if he knows what I'm thinking, Silver nuzzles his snout against my leg as we walk. Glancing down at him, I smile and brush the top of his head with my fingertips.

You'll always be my family, I tell him with a look.

"We have a choice to make," Dad announces cheerily, as he and Lucy catch up with us. He holds out the paper map he insists on using instead of a phone app and which he's been eagerly checking ever since we stepped off the train. "The trail splits here and we can either go left" – he gestures to the woodland that way – "or we can go right." He points the other way to the path that crosses an open field. "Now, it's completely up to you, but I do believe there's a river that runs through the woods. Apparently, there's a very pretty waterfall to be found in there, too, not to mention a famous old, rickety bridge. You're not allowed to walk across it any more as it's become too dangerous, but I read that it's a great spot for a photo. The path through the field leads to the village, which is meant to be nice, but, you know" – his eyes glint with adventure – "probably less fun."

"I have a feeling you want us to go into the woods!" Lucy laughs, wrapping her arm around Dad's waist.

"I don't mind what we do!" Dad insists, before hesitating. "Although, now you mention it, the woods do look very mysterious and intriguing."

"I vote we go into the woods," I say, as Lucy winks at me behind Dad's back.

"Me too." Kieron nods.

"Woods it is," Lucy declares, causing Dad's expression to brighten.

"Come on, then!" he instructs, stepping past us and leading the way into the trees. "I think the animals will be happier with this route. Lots more to explore in here."

Dad may have a point: Blizzard and Stripes race off ahead of us to run about the woodland floor, pouncing through the ferns and mosses, while Talon swoops and flits round the tall trunks, dancing in the beams of sunshine breaking through the branches and leaves. Chomp remains on my shoulder and I quietly promise him that I'll find a nice rocky area for him around the waterfall Dad mentioned.

"It's a shame your nan couldn't come today," Kieron says, falling back into step with me as we follow Dad.

"Clementine isn't exactly a fan of nature," Lucy reminds her son with a chuckle. "She can barely stand a speck of dirt in her house. Can you imagine what she'd think of all this mud?"

"Surely she's grown used to a bit of mess now that she lives with a dog, a cat, a ferret, a gecko *and* a sparrow," Kieron lists wearily.

"I'm not so sure," I say, thinking back to her reaction yesterday when she got home from aerial yoga and Dad had to fill her in on Blizzard's misadventure with the trifle. I hid at the top of the stairs.

"She loves the animals in her own way," Lucy reasons. "It's not easy adopting so many all at once, especially when you're not exactly … uh … *fond* of pets in the first place."

"I am lucky that Nan agreed to let them live with us," I say. "Mum was never allowed a pet growing up, no matter how much she begged."

"And these aren't exactly your average pets either," Kieron adds, glancing to Silver as he swiftly hops over a fallen tree branch strewn across the path.

"Yeah, if you thought dogs shed hair, try hoovering up after a wolf," I say.

"They only transform when you're in trouble, though, right?" Lucy checks.

"Well, technically, those are the only times I've

30

needed them to transform," I explain, sharing a look with Kieron, who attempts to hide his smirk. "But I've done a few practice rounds with them at home, just to make sure that everything is in order."

Lucy stops on the path to face me, crossing her arms.

"Are you telling me that Clementine has had to put up with a polar bear stomping around her house?" she asks.

"Polar bears don't really stomp," I correct her.

"Yeah, they have a kind of lumbering, rolling gait, and because their heels touch the ground first, it's quite a soft plod," Kieron adds. "Unless they're charging at something, in which case, I would say that—"

Lucy holds up her hand to interrupt him. "My point is, I'm a huge animal fan – so huge, I have dedicated my life to rescuing them – and not even I would really appreciate a polar bear roaming about my house, soft plod or not."

"I think she has more of an issue with the crocodile," I say thoughtfully, reaching up to tickle

Chomp's chin. "You see, even when they smile innocently at you, it still looks a bit threatening."

"It's all those teeth," Kieron says, wincing involuntarily.

Lucy lets out a heavy sigh. "Poor Clementine."

"It's not forever. Dad is finding us a new house, remember?" I point out.

"I suppose." She hesitates. "But still, it's not exactly ideal for you and your dad, either; a crocodile in your living room."

Our conversation is interrupted by a piercing scream that echoes through the woods. I swivel round and Dad's head snaps up from studying his map.

"What was that?" Kieron asks.

"It sounds like someone's in trouble!" Lucy exclaims as we hear another yelp.

Consulting his map once more, Dad gulps, his face going pale.

"It's coming from the waterfall," he says.

"Let's go!" I cry.

Without wasting any time, I run as fast as I can, and Silver, Stripes and Blizzard pelt down the path in front of me, while Talon soars overhead. Within moments I can hear the sound of rushing water nearby. Passing an ancient, wonky wooden arrow pointing me in the right direction, I emerge from the trees into a clearing. Straight ahead is an old rope bridge suspended across a picturesque waterfall flowing into a fast-paced river below.

Strewn out on the grass next to the various unmissable warning signs, stating in bold capital letters that access to the bridge is strictly prohibited, are three bikes. One of the boys who sped past us earlier is standing with the bikes next to the cliff edge, his hands covering his mouth in fright.

Noticing me, he holds out a shaking hand and points at the middle of the bridge.

"They're… They're going to fall!" he yells. "We dared each other to cross it to the other side! It was just a joke!"

One of his friends is hanging from the bridge still

wearing his backpack, his legs dangling through a gap where some of the wooden decking has given way, clinging on and screaming for help. The other is lying flat on his front, unable to reach his friend, his hands gripping the sides of the wooden decking, looking frozen in fear as the bridge wobbles and sways.

At a gust of wind, the bridge creaks angrily.

"Help me! *Please!*" cries the boy hanging from the middle, while the other whimpers.

Without any instruction, Talon swoops down to

land on my shoulder next to Chomp; Stripes jumps on to my foot and Blizzard runs up my leg, leaping into my cradled arms. Silver leans against my leg, looking up at me with his glassy golden eyes, ready for action. Taking a deep breath, I close my eyes and shut out the world, focusing on the magic of the pendant hanging round my neck.

There's a burst of light, bathing the woods in a shimmering blue glow.

The boy waiting on the verge gasps, his eyes growing wide, as in front of him appears a roaring tiger, a magnificent polar bear, a snapping crocodile and a striking wolf, while a dazzling eagle flies through the air.

They all look to me with their luminous golden eyes. I know that mine are now shining the same colour.

Let's go, I tell them, without having to say a word.

Chomp crawls down the bank, navigating the steep drop all the way to the river, where he slinks into the water and positions himself directly under the boys, ready to act as a safety net. Hastening to the edge of the cliff, Blizzard lets out an almighty roar and uses his two heavy front paws to pin down the edge of the bridge and pull it towards him gradually, tightening the ropes and steadying the structure.

Agile and breathtakingly graceful, Stripes hops round Blizzard to begin slowly slinking her way down the bridge towards the first boy. My breath catches in my throat as the wood panels creak beneath her added weight, but she doesn't flinch, letting out a determined growl as she ducks her head and keeps her body low, crawling closer to him. Approaching his feet, she stops and lifts her front right paw, her razor-sharp claws glinting in the sunshine.

With one swift movement, she swipes her paw at the boy and flings him on to her back. He lets out a yelp of surprise as he lands, before wrapping his arms tightly around her neck. Deftly turning, Stripes leaps back on to the grass, comforting the boy with a gentle purr to let him know that he's safe now.

Meanwhile, Talon has flown to his friend, who is

becoming more and more panicked, losing his grip on the bridge as he desperately digs his fingers into the wood panel from which he's hanging. Hovering next to him, Talon waits until Silver is in position, signalling to her that he's ready by throwing his head back and howling.

Stretching her long, muscular legs forward as she swoops behind the boy, Talon's curved, razor-sharp claws grab at his backpack just as he lets go of the bridge, unable to hold on any more. Screaming as he drops, he finds himself flying through the air as Talon catches him and with all her strength, tosses him to Silver, who quickly moves so that the boy lands with a soft thud on his back.

With a sob of relief, the boy buries his face into Silver's fur.

I whoop loudly, punching the air.

We did it! I communicate, beaming at the animals as Talon soars upwards to do a celebratory somersault and Stripes lets out a triumphant roar.

But when I turn to smile at the third friend, who

never made it on to the bridge, my heart sinks. He's holding his phone up, filming everything. Amazed, he points the camera directly at me.

"You need to delete that video," I tell him urgently, taking a step forwards.

He frowns, lowering his phone. "I… I can't."

"Please, it's really important that you do!"

"No, I *can't*," he emphasizes nervously. "I'm live."

Silver looks at me, his golden eyes filled with worry.

Our secret is out.

CHAPTER THREE

It turns out that there is something that can annoy Nan more than a ferret causing havoc in her kitchen: the paparazzi ruining her front lawn.

Ever since the incident at the bridge, reporters have been swarming around the front of the house, desperate to speak to me and get photographs of the animals. I don't know how they tracked us down, but they arrived at Nan's front door within the hour of the video being streamed online and when Dad and I arrived home from the walk, there was an eruption of noise as they shoved microphones under my nose and shouted questions over each other so I couldn't hear any of them. It was overwhelming and made me feel claustrophobic. I couldn't see where I was going because of all the camera flashes going off in my face, making my eyesight go all splodgy.

Dad put his arm around me protectively and, holding me close, attempted to bulldoze through them to get to the door. They were so determined, he found it tricky at first, but as soon as Silver growled at them, the crowd parted.

"That's the w-wolf!" one of them cried, prompting the lot of them to jump back to let us through, suddenly jittery but intrigued enough not to run away.

It's been three days since they arrived and they're still all out there, camping overnight on the road, staying put just in case I emerge from the house with the animals and give them the story they're after. I've been too apprehensive to leave the house, peering carefully through the curtain every now and then to check if they've given up and gone home. I spent the afternoon after the incident trawling through social media, reading the thousands of comments as the world began to give its opinion. Most people are in awe of the animals, some are terrified, and others think it's all a hoax.

The biggest worry is: I know that somewhere out there, the boss of Magnitude – whoever they are – is already plotting to steal them back.

I've been so worried about the safety of the animals, I've barely slept.

"Look at them!" Nan cries on Wednesday morning, peeking through a crack in the blinds of her living room and then putting her hands on her hips.

Curled up on her sofa, I hug my knees to my chest. Silver is lying on the floor next to me and Chomp is having a snooze on the cushion by my feet, while Stripes and Blizzard scamper about the middle of the room, playing with a mouse toy that Nan bought for Stripes and that Blizzard loves to steal. Talon is out in the garden, hiding from the noise.

"Do those journalists care about my grass? No, they don't!" Nan continues, grumpily. "Do they care about my petunias? No, they don't! You'd think by now they'd have got the message that we're not interested in talking to them. Why don't they focus on writing about that tiara instead?"

"What tiara?" I ask.

"It was the second lead story in the news – there's been the most amazing discovery," she begins, her eyes lighting up with intrigue. "There was a fire at an old country house – or mansion, I should say – in Oxfordshire and while they were doing the repairs, they discovered a box hidden in the walls, and you'll never guess what it contained!"

I blink at her. "A tiara?"

"Gave that away a bit, didn't I?" She chuckles. "Yes. Although, it wasn't just any tiara, but one of great historic importance. Experts think that it may have belonged to Queen Elizabeth the first! Isn't that extraordinary? To think it's been sitting there, buried away in that house all this time."

"Wow, that is a cool discovery, and a much more interesting story than me." I sigh, hearing the reporters chatting outside.

"They're going to put the tiara on display in London and apparently they'll be inviting royal families from all over the world to come see it on a grand opening night." Nan glances over at me. "I read celebrities and high-profile figures will be invited too – you might make the list now, Luna."

I snort. "Yeah, sure, Nan."

"Why not? You'd be top of *my* invite list."

"Thanks, Nan. If only you were in charge of everything."

"I'll say."

Glancing out the window, she gasps.

"You know what I've just seen, Luna? One of the photographers has dropped a receipt on the ground reaching for something in his pocket and he hasn't picked it up. He's seen it fall and he's just shrugged and left it! He's littering! In my neighbourhood! Well, I won't stand for that."

She marches out the room and I hear her bustling about in the kitchen. I watch as she storms down the hall past the living room doorway towards the front door, carrying a recycling bin bag. She throws open the front door, prompting a flurry of excitement from the reporters who swarm to the step to greet her.

"You there! Young man, you with the big fancy camera hanging round your neck!" I hear her say. "Yes, you! You dropped that receipt on the ground. Don't look sheepish, I saw it fall from your pocket! Pick it up at once and put it in here. That's right. Good. Don't apologize to me, young man, apologize to the planet! Apologize to the neighbours! This is a community. You respect it and you respect the earth. Keep this bag and share it amongst you for all your recycling. I'll fetch you other bags for the rest of your rubbish. I expect this road to be spotless when you

45

finally give up and go home, is that understood?"

There's a small rumbling of murmurs.

"I said, *is that understood*?" Nan repeats, authoritatively.

"Yes," the reporters chorus in a much more enthusiastic manner.

"Good," she states, satisfied. "And mind my grass! Look at you lot, treading all over it. Do any of you have a garden? Would you want the grass to be turned to mud from a group of people trampling all over it? No, I didn't think so. I'm sure some of you grow very pretty flowers, too? Then you know the time and care that goes into a garden. I'd appreciate it if you respect my borders. If I see one more petunia suffering from your presence, I'll get *really* cross. Would you like me to get *really* cross?"

"No," comes the nervous response.

"I didn't think so," she huffs, before letting out a sigh. "Now, since you insist on lurking, I might as well make you all some tea."

"Actually, Clementine, any chance of sampling

some red pea soup?" a journalist asks hopefully. "One of your neighbours said it was the kind of food that's life changing."

"It certainly is," she confirms. "But I won't be cooking you any of that while you're hounding my granddaughter." She pauses, waiting for the groans of disappointment to die down. "Now, hands up for tea."

The door shuts and she goes to put the kettle on. Letting out a heavy sigh, I reach out to where Silver is sitting and stroke his head. Stripes gives up on trying to get the mouse toy back from Blizzard and stalks across the room to me, hopping up gracefully and curling up on my lap. Blizzard looks disappointed in her ending the game and tries to get Silver to join in with him by nudging the mouse toy towards him hopefully. Silver gives him a stern look that tells him he's not in a playful mood.

"Sorry that we haven't been able to go on any long walks since Sunday," I announce to the four of them. "I know that you hate being cooped up in here. I don't like it, either."

Silver lifts his head and rests his chin on my arm. I smile gratefully at him.

The doorbell goes and Nan begins muttering about the audacity of the reporters, calling out that tea will be ready in a minute. When it rings once more, she comes thundering down the hallway again to the front door and, even though I really don't like the reporters hovering by the house, I genuinely feel sorry for them. They have no idea the lecture coming their way.

"I told you that… Oh! Hello," I hear Nan say in surprise once the door has been opened. "Come in, come in!"

"Thank you, I'm sorry to disturb you," comes the reply, a woman's voice I don't recognize. "I hope those journalists aren't bothering you too much."

"Nothing we can't handle," Nan says.

"I'm pleased to hear it. I wonder if I might have a word with Luna Wolf?"

"Of course! She's through here."

Nan comes into the living room and behind her

48

follows a woman dressed in a smart, speckless police uniform, carrying her hat in her hand and her dark hair scraped back into a tight bun, not a strand out of place. She looks stern and authoritative, unlike the clumsy young police officer who has accompanied her, tripping over his own feet as he steps through the door, apologizing profusely as he knocks over a vase on one of the coffee tables, catching it just before it smashes. Carefully placing it back where it was, he flinches at the withering look he receives from his companion.

"Luna Wolf, what an honour to meet you. I'm Chief Superintendent Reece," the woman announces, holding out her hand for me to shake as I jump to my feet at her entrance. She gestures to the officer next to her. "This is Constable Croft."

"Hi," I say, bewildered. "Am I in trouble?"

"Not today," she informs me matter-of-factly. "I have a proposition for you that I'd like to discuss."

"Please sit down, Chief Superintendent," Nan offers.

"That's quite all right, I prefer standing." She sniffs, jutting out her chin. "It provides opportunity for working on good posture."

Both Constable Croft and I straighten our backs and pull back our shoulders at her pointed comment.

"I was making a pot of tea for the reporters," Nan says. "Can I offer either of you a cup?"

"Not while we're on the job, thank you. We only drink water while working, isn't that right, Constable Croft?"

He nods dismally. "Yes, that's right. We're not allowed anything enjoyable that might distract us in any way from doing the best policing possible."

"I see." Nan raises her eyebrows. "Can I fetch you a glass of water then?"

"No time for such indulgence, thank you," Chief Superintendent Reece says in a clipped manner. "I'll get straight to the point, Miss Wolf. I'm here on official business. It has come to our attention that you are in possession of..." She hesitates, her eyes flickering to the animals surrounding me, all

50

watching her with great curiosity. "Creatures with extraordinary powers."

"They're *amazing*!" gushes Constable Croft.

Chief Superintendent Reece shoots him a sharp glare over her shoulder and he apologetically bows his head and looks at the ground, his cheeks flushing.

"As I was saying, these animals have some intriguing abilities," she continues, "and we think that, should you be interested in public duty, they might be able to help us."

"Help you?" I ask, confused. "As in … help the police?"

"Not just the police, but all public services: fire department, ambulances, lifeguard assistance," she lists. "As far as I can tell, these animals have great potential. With a little direction, order and discipline, they could save many lives. What do you think?"

I blink at her. "Uh… I…"

"Are you asking Luna to join the police force?" Nan asks, jumping in as I struggle to form a sentence.

"Of course not, she's much too young," Chief

Superintendent Reece states, lines forming on her forehead. "I'm proposing that, in certain dire circumstances when lives are at risk, she loans us the animals to help."

"I can't do that," I say quickly, placing a hand on Silver's head. "I mean, I would love to help others, but I can't just loan the animals out. They only transform for me."

"That's something that can be easily worked around," she insists. "You could accompany them to the sites to which they are called. We will give you this radio scanner" – she clicks her fingers and Constable Croft quickly fumbles in his pocket for what looks like a walkie-talkie, handing it to me – "and when you hear us say certain code words, you will know that we are calling for your help."

"Like the bat signal in Batman," Constable Croft adds excitedly. "But instead of shining the bat symbol into the sky, we'd call out a phrase and you'd come to the rescue!"

Chief Superintendent Reece clears her throat

impatiently and he steps back again, whispering an apology.

"Yes, like the bat signal," she repeats, unimpressed.

"What would the phrase be?" I ask, examining the radio.

"We discussed it at length and landed on, 'Code Wolf'," she announces proudly. "Should you hear someone say 'Code Wolf', you know we're in need of your help on whatever rescue mission is taking place. What do you think? Will you help us?"

I rub my forehead. "I wasn't really expecting any of this. The animals' superpowers are meant to be a secret."

Chief Superintendent Reece marches over to the curtains and pulls one slightly open, looking out at the horde of paparazzi waiting outside.

"It's a little late for that, Miss Wolf," she says, pulling the curtain closed again.

"I know. I didn't mean for this to happen," I say glumly, slumping back down on the sofa, feeling deflated. "I'm meant to keep them safe."

"I understand that this is a big undertaking; we're asking a lot of you," Chief Superintendent Reece says, her voice softening slightly. "You don't have to agree, of course, but we wanted to pitch it as a collaboration that would do a lot of good. Your animals could really make a difference with—"

She's interrupted by a crackled voice that comes out of Constable Croft's radio, demanding his attention. Constable Croft presses a button and speaks back.

"Croft here. What's going on?"

"Incident in the River Lea near Tottenham," comes the reply. "All units nearby respond. All units nearby respond. Over."

"That's down the road!" Nan repeats, her expression wrought with concern.

Receiving a nod from Chief Superintendent Reece, Constable Croft talks again into his radio. "Croft here, we will report at once. Any more information about the incident?"

"From what we can tell, an escapologist, Mr

Frederick Flair, has got himself in some kind of trouble during an attempt to escape from a glass box in the water and needs urgent assistance. Over."

"Oh my goodness!" Nan gasps, placing a hand on her heart. "I watched a TV show about Frederick Flair and his endurance feats just the other day. The way he dismounted from a trapeze while blindfolded so elegantly inspired my own aerial yoga style!"

"Trapped in a glass box in water – I can't imagine he has much time," Chief Superintendent Reece remarks, her brow furrowed. "Miss Wolf, I know you haven't made your decision, but it sounds like Frederick Flair could really use your help."

She and Constable Croft look at me with hopeful expressions. I bite my lip, feeling torn, anxiously twirling my pendant round my fingers. Silver nudges my hand and I gaze down into his golden eyes. I know what he's telling me.

Someone is in danger. He needs us.

"What do you say, Luna?" The Chief Superintendent prompts. "Code Wolf?"

I take a deep breath and jump to my feet, the animals following my lead and instantly standing to attention.

"Code Wolf," I confirm with a determined nod. "Let's go."

A huge crowd is gathered by the water when we arrive. Some of the audience look relaxed and suspicious, clearly under the impression that all of the panic surrounding the stunt is part of the trick to build momentum to a more satisfying finish. Others are kicking off their shoes, preparing to get in the water.

Jumping out of the police car with all the animals in tow, I rush to the edge of the bank just in time to see the top of a glass box sink below the surface. A woman with long flaming red hair tied up in a high ponytail and wearing a black sequin suit comes rushing over to us, tears streaming down her face.

"This isn't meant to happen!" she cries, pointing at the box as it disappears below the surface. "He's meant to have broken free of his handcuffs by this point, but something went wrong as he was trying to reach the key. I think he fainted! You have to help him!"

"We're going to do everything we can," Chief Superintendent Reece assures her. "You're his assistant, I presume?"

"Yes, I'm Kelly," she sobs. "There's an air hole at the top of the glass, which is now going to be filling the box with water! Please help him."

"Can he smash the glass somehow if the cold water wakes him?" Constable Croft asks, panicked.

Kelly shakes her head. "It's meant to be unbreakable!"

"Kelly, you said that he couldn't reach the key in time to break free of his handcuffs," I ask her urgently. "Where is the key?"

"It's taped to the outside of the top of the box, next to the door hatch," she says, fanning her face dramatically with her hand. "He *promised* me that he practiced this yesterday, but I *knew* he was wasting his time trying to complete that Rubik's cube his mum bought him. And now look! It's a total DISASTER!"

"Luna, I don't know how—" Chief Inspector Reece begins, but I interrupt.

"I have a plan," I assure her.

I turn to face the animals, who quickly move close so they can prepare to transform. As Constable Croft attempts to take control of the audience and usher them back out of the way, I can hear their excited whispers and gasps as they notice me. Trying not to allow myself to be distracted and overwhelmed by the pressure of the situation, I feel the warmth of Silver's fur underneath my hand, comforted by his belief in me as I close my eyes and will the magic to work.

The blue light bursts from the pendant and a breeze from Talon's eagle wings brushes my cheek as she pushes off from my shoulder and soars into the sky. The crowd gasp in amazement at the sight of Blizzard becoming a polar bear and roaring with determination, while Silver joins in in his wolf form, letting out a long howl. Stripes, now a tiger, swishes her tail and Chomp nudges my ankle with his long, pointed crocodile snout, ready for action as the strongest and speediest swimmer.

I calmly and quickly communicate what I need them to do, the magic connecting our thoughts. Blizzard and Chomp crawl into the water and, with all his might, Chomp propels Blizzard down to the glass box in a flash. Once he's reached it, Blizzard is able to use his mighty polar bear strength to lift the box towards the surface. Meanwhile, Chomp starts slamming himself against the glass in the hope that the thuds will wake up Frederick Flair.

The top of the box resurfaces and the crowd cheers, but our work is far from over.

Talon, it's your turn, I tell her.

As a soaked Frederick Flair regains consciousness and quickly realizes what's going on, the eagle swoops down to the top of the box, where she uses her talons to swipe at the tape strapping the key on to the box and knocking it down through the airhole.

Frederick tries to feel for it, but it's no easy feat – his hands are cuffed behind his back and there's water in the box now, making the key slosh about, slipping through this grasp.

My throat begins to feel tight and I will Blizzard to come up for air. He resists at first, but as soon as Frederick cries out, "GOT IT!", Blizzard carefully lowers the box and Chomp helps push him up quickly to the surface. As I see the shiny black nose of my polar bear break the water and gulp in some air, I feel able to breathe again myself.

Satisfied that Blizzard is OK, Chomp dives once more to help Frederick open the door hatch, which is made difficult by the pressure of the water. Silver paddles in and, once Chomp has managed to pry the door back and prop it open with his jaw, Frederick swims up to the wolf, throwing his arms around his neck, allowing Silver to carry him to where Stripes is waiting on the bank. She uses her tiger claws to hook the back of his spandex costume and hoist Frederick out of the water, before quickly curling herself around him, making him warm and cosy as he shivers from the shock.

I breathe a sigh of relief and, now that I know Frederick Flair is safe, allow myself to enjoy the smug expression on my dry tiger's face as she watches Silver shake out his fur.

No matter how big and ferocious they are, cats do hate water.

I'm so engrossed in my animals' thoughts and feelings as they each climb safely out of the water that I don't notice the deafening cheers of the audience straight away, or the number of camera phones pointing at us, capturing every moment. Thankfully, the crowd soon disperses as ambulances and paramedics make their way through.

"Thank you, Luna Wolf," Frederick Flair whispers, giving me a weak smile as he remains snuggled into Stripes's fur. "Your super animals saved my life."

Silver comes to sit next to me and I rest my hand on his head, a warm fuzzy feeling filling my belly.

"I'd say our first Code Wolf was a great success, wouldn't you?" Chief Superintendent Reece declares, after instructing Constable Croft to start taking statements. "I look forward to working together in the future."

"Me too."

She hesitates. "You know, Luna, when I joined the police force here in London, I never imagined that one day I'd be working alongside a polar bear, a crocodile, a tiger, a wolf and an eagle."

Letting out a sigh, a smile spreads across her face before she continues, "It all goes to show that no matter how old you are or where you've ended up, life can still surprise you in the most wonderful of ways."

CHAPTER FOUR

The interview was Kieron's idea.

"We need to take control of the narrative," he had informed me bossily one afternoon, when I'd just had to battle my way through the paparazzi to the front door again. "The media has taken the story and run with it; they can say what they like because they don't have the facts. If you let me interview you, you can tell them the truth. Once you've told your story, there will be nothing else for them to write about. The interest in you and the animals will start to die down and things can go back to normal. Sort of."

I knew he was right, which was why I agreed

to let him do the interview. Things were getting completely out of control. The bridge incident brought us attention, but after we successfully rescued Frederick Flair, our popularity went stratospheric.

Frederick Flair didn't exactly help matters, either. He's been on every single news channel discussing his "brush with death" and the "miracle super animals" that saved his life. He sent so many thank-you flowers to Nan's house that every room has become a bizarre obstacle course with vases threatening to trip you up at every step. He's even asked if he can have the rights to the story to work with a Hollywood crew to turn it into a film.

Nan told him we'd consider it, but our decision would largely hang on which actress would be chosen to play her.

"I want final casting decision!" she told him in no uncertain terms.

He hastily agreed.

I've hardly had time to take it all in, all this change and unwanted attention. I've been much too busy the past few days rushing around London on rescue missions with the animals, ignoring the bystanders who film or photograph us for social media, and each rescue seems to go viral.

There was the teenager we rescued from the Thames after he'd jumped in to retrieve his new phone that he'd accidentally dropped in the water while taking a selfie on the South Bank; the jewel thief we helped after she got in a spot of bother trying to scale the Tower of London; the inventor who needed us to rush to his aid when his gigantic robot caught on fire and started uncontrollably stomping around Oxford Circus; and the group of tourists we escorted safely from the London Dungeons after their enraged tour operator got tired of their constant questions and locked them all down there before running away with the only key.

The animals are suddenly famous and, unfortunately, so am I. Everywhere I go, someone is pointing a phone at me and the press remains camped outside Nan's door. I've found it all very overwhelming – although there is one silver lining: I've received an invite to the unveiling of the recently discovered royal tiara on its grand opening night. I'm allowed to bring someone with me, so I've invited Nan.

"Are you sure, Luna?" she'd gasped with excitement when I asked her. "Don't you want to bring one of your friends?"

"You told me I was top of your invite list, remember? Well, you're top of mine," I'd explained simply.

She'd enveloped me in the biggest hug and immediately started to worry out loud about what she'd wear to the occasion and whether it would be appropriate to bring a Tupperware of salt-fish fritters for all the royalty in attendance to try.

Glamorous invites aside, I know that Dad is getting worried about me having to fend off all the attention – he's told me not to read any comments online and warned me to stay away from social media – but I can't give up on these rescue missions now. These people need help and we have the power to help them. If "Code Wolf" comes through on the radio, we are out the door like a shot, no matter how many reporters yell questions at us on the way. I can't let everyone down just because it's hard. As Chief Superintendent Reece pointed out, we are making a difference.

But as we've become more and more famous, we've somehow courted more and more controversy. Dad can try to protect me all he likes, but I've read what people are saying about me – the bad as well as the good. Some people are starting to think that I'm some kind of evil genius. Others are even accusing me of being an alien from outer space, which I find insulting, but Kieron thinks is hilarious.

"What a boring alien. No offence," he'd said, after we watched a breakfast show where they'd invited someone on to the sofa to discuss her theory about me coming from another planet. "You land on Earth and what do you do? Move to Tottenham, help out at a dog and cat rescue centre and spend your evenings eating entire pots of ice cream."

"Hey! That was one time," I'd huffed.

He'd laughed and later that day, when I'd returned home from popping to the shops with Nan, which ended up taking about two hours thanks to everyone wanting selfies with me, he'd brought up the interview idea.

After discussing it with Dad, Lucy and Nan, I agreed that it might be handy to set the story straight, especially as the attention didn't seem to be dying down. The animals and I were still on every front page. Kieron double-checked it was the smart thing to do by emailing Rex Robinson and asking him his opinion on the matter. According to Kieron, Rex replied speedily, giving his approval.

So, the day before I start at my new school, I sit down on Nan's sofa with Kieron, ready to tell him my story. All the family and animals are here with me, even Talon, who is perched once again in her favourite spot: on Nan's head.

"OK, we're all set," Kieron says, setting up his camera on a tripod and taking his spot on the kitchen

chair he's placed next to it. "As discussed, we're going to keep this short and simple. Just a few questions about you, the animals and their superpowers, and why the rescue missions are important to you. Are you feeling all right?"

Swallowing the lump in my throat, I nod. Silver, sitting to attention at my feet, nudges my leg with his nose in solidarity. Stripes is keeping my lap warm, Blizzard is wrapped round my neck, and Chomp is on my right shoulder. Before we start, Talon launches herself from Nan's hair and comes flitting over to land on my left shoulder.

Ruffling her feathers, she tweets indignantly.

"Yeah," I whisper to her, "I wish we didn't have to do this either."

"You're going to be great, Luna," Dad says, sitting with Nan behind the camera.

"Yeah, you've got this," Lucy tells me warmly.

"Thanks," I say, resting a hand on Silver's head. "I'm really glad you're all here."

"Always," Nan states.

"And you're certain you want to stream this live to my blog?" Kieron checks, lifting his head from examining the list of questions he's got printed out in front of him.

"Definitely," I say. "I don't want anyone accusing us of weird editing."

"OK, well, remember that even though all the best journalists are neutral and devoted to an unbiased and impartial delivery of relevant facts and information … I must admit that I'm on your side," Kieron says with a mischievous smile. "But don't tell anyone I said that."

I smile back at him. "I promise."

"Great. Now, deep breath," he instructs.

Looking past him at Nan, who joins in to steady my breathing, we inhale deeply and then exhale audibly together. She gives me an encouraging nod.

"Ready?" Kieron asks, reaching out to his camera.

I look directly into the lens.

"Ready."

It's strange to start at a new school when everyone already knows who you are. The moment I step into the main building on that first Monday, I can feel everyone staring at me and whispering with each other in their clusters of friends. Sticking close to Kieron's side as he guides me down the corridor to the head teacher's office, my face grows hot with embarrassment and I keep my head down, eyes on my feet.

The interview with Kieron has been a success, as far as we can tell – the feedback overnight has been mostly positive and when Dad and I left the house this morning, there were definitely fewer reporters lingering. Now that I'd said everything that needed to be said, there was no chance of an exclusive or interesting comment. They'd given up to go chase another story.

I can only hope the other students here at school will lose interest quickly, too.

"No need to introduce yourself," declares Ms Sanderson, the head of the school, as she comes rushing round her desk to shake my hand. "What an honour to have you join our student body, Luna!"

"Thank you," I say quietly, my cheeks burning.

"You know, if you like I can bend the rules for you," she tells me conspiratorially, nudging my arm with her elbow, "and allow you to bring the animals to class. I'm sure they're well enough behaved to join you here on campus!"

"That's all right, thanks, I'll leave them at home," I reply, horrified at the idea of drawing any more attention during my first week.

It was awful saying goodbye to them this morning

when I left the house, especially Silver. But it's the right thing to do for all of us – I have to face school on my own. And Ms Sanderson assured Chief Superintendent Reece that I could keep the police radio with me at all times, so if anything terrible happens and the animals are needed, I won't miss it.

"Shame, I would so love to have met them." Ms Sanderson sighs. "Don't hesitate to ask if you want to bring them in so we can all meet the famous Super Animal Adventurers!"

That's the name one of the newspapers gave us: "The Super Animal Adventurers". It's terrible, in my opinion, but annoyingly, it's caught on. Even Frederick Flair has called Nan to ask her if he can use that as a working title for his screenplay.

I thought that going to a new school would be hard because I never really fit in, but I think it might be even worse going to school when all you do is stand out. My first day is a total disaster. I'm hardly in any of the same classes as Kieron, so I have to suffer everyone's unsubtle pointed looks on my own, and when I finally get to spend time with him at lunch, no one comes near us except to ask for a selfie with me. The teachers do their best to keep the students focused on the lessons, but it proves difficult and is made even worse when the police radio goes off.

"It's a Code Wolf!" exclaims a boy in my class, sending everyone into a frenzy of excitement as they pelt me with questions about the rescue mission. Except there isn't one, because it's a false alarm, and the teacher spends the next fifteen minutes trying to get everyone to settle down while I sink lower and lower into my chair, clutching my pendant and wishing for time to go quicker.

After the last bell rings for the day, I don't hang around to meet Kieron but run home as fast as I can to the animals, burying my face in Silver's neck as soon as I'm through the door and telling him that I never want to leave the house again.

"So your first day at school was difficult," Nan says over dinner that evening, despite the fact I haven't said a word. Somehow, she always knows. "Don't worry, Luna. It will get better. Give it time."

"I'm not so sure," I mutter, taking comfort in the delicious Caribbean fish pie she's served.

"You remember when you first moved to London and I told you to be patient and you'd find your feet here soon? You weren't so sure then either." She chuckles, ladling some more food on to my plate. "Tomorrow will be brighter, you wait and see."

I try to trust in her words, but walking to school the next day feels like I'm wading through treacle, a sinking feeling of dread filling my stomach as I reach the gates and Dad waves me off with a fixed smile on his face.

Taking a seat at a desk in the back in my form room ready for registration, I keep my eyes fixed on looking out the window, trying to pretend like I don't notice the group of people in the far corner of the room whispering and stealing glances at me.

"Hey."

I jump at the voice in my ear, spinning round in

my seat to find a girl has slid into the chair next to me. Her long blonde hair is tied back in a ponytail. She's petite with delicate features and big curious eyes, her school bag covered in colourful badges, several of them promoting environmental charities.

"Hi," I say warily.

"I'm Ivy," she states, smiling warmly at me. "You're Luna, right?"

I nod.

"I thought I'd come over and say hi because I noticed all of yesterday that no one actually did that. I guess they're all too nervous; it's like you're a celebrity or something," she explains breezily, reaching in her bag for her books and pencil case. "But I figured that if I were at a new school, I'd want someone to come say hi, whether I was a celebrity or not. Tell me if you want me to go away and I can leave you alone."

"No, no," I say hurriedly. "It's nice to have someone to sit with."

"Cool. So, how are you finding it here? Aside

76

from feeling like a goldfish in a bowl," she notes, giving the whispering group nearby an unimpressed, pointed look. They quickly stop talking and turn away.

"It's… Uh … well…"

"Yeah, I thought as much," she says as I trail off. "Don't worry. I was new last year and your first week can't be worse than mine."

"Why? What happened?" I ask, intrigued.

She sighs. "I fell into a bin."

I burst out laughing. "You *what*?"

"I fell into a bin," she repeats. "I was watching a really interesting video on my phone about the decline of the orangutan population because of deforestation in south-east Asia, and I wasn't looking where I was going. Next thing know, I'm tumbling head first into a bin, and then I'm stuck upside down. Anyway, since then I haven't looked at my phone while walking. Head up at all times. I recommend it."

"Thanks for the tip," I say, still chuckling.

"So there you go, as difficult as your day is, it could be worse. You could be stuck in a bin and have Mrs Hutch attempting to pull you out by your ankles."

"I guess that would be worse." I smile warmly at her. "Thanks, Ivy."

"For what?"

"I don't know." I shrug. "Talking to me normally."

"Everyone knows how scary it is to be new," she says matter-of-factly. "And you have to deal with all the media stuff on top of that…" She pauses, frowning at me before continuing: "I'm really sorry that they won't leave you alone. It must be horrible, reporters following you everywhere."

"It's not very fun."

She shakes her head angrily. "They're the worst. I hope they leave you alone soon. I'm so sorry."

"It's not your fault!"

She nods. "Anyway, forget all of them. This is probably stating the obvious, but you like animals, right?"

"Yeah, I like animals."

"Then let me find you this amazing video about orangutans," she insists, getting out her phone and typing into it.

I smile as she holds out the clip for me to watch.

Nan was right. Things feel brighter already.

CHAPTER FIVE

When Nan declared that she was going to host one of her famous gatherings with all our family, Kieron suggested we invite Ivy, and Nan thought it was a brilliant idea.

"Of course!" she'd cried, whilst shooing Chomp away from the freshly baked cookies she'd made specially for Kieron, setting them down in front of him. "You must invite your new friend. Just because I call it a family lunch, that doesn't mean it's exclusively for 'family'. Everyone is welcome!"

Kieron and I had shared a knowing smile – when Nan says that everyone is welcome, she means it.

The whole street often turns up to her parties, some of them without knowing that she's even hosting an event — they just smell her cooking while they're passing and ring the doorbell hopefully. Before moving to London, the idea of a crowded party terrified me, but since living with Nan, I've had to grow used to it. Thankfully I now have the animals to help me feel more at ease — without them, I'd have continued hiding up in my room, avoiding the barrage of questions that is usually pelted at me by my distant relations.

I wasn't sure Ivy would want to come to our family lunch, but when I asked her at school, she'd accepted enthusiastically.

"I should warn you that you'd be meeting my entire family," I'd emphasized strongly. "There are a *lot* of them."

"Sounds fun!" she'd exclaimed, and she'd sounded like she meant it and wasn't just being polite. "Thanks so much, Luna, I can't wait! I'll be there."

"Do you need to check with your parents that you can come?"

She'd blushed and looked away, shaking her head.

"I live with my dad. He won't mind, it's all good," she'd said, before changing the subject.

Since I first started chatting to Ivy on my second day we've become friends, which seems amazing to me. At my last school, I didn't have *one* close friend – they all thought I was a big freak, lost in a daydream most of the time and too shy to join in any conversation – but I've only been at this school a couple of weeks now and I can claim to have two proper friends: Kieron and now Ivy. When I mentioned to Kieron last week that Ivy had been really nice to me in class, he'd seemed impressed.

"Ivy Campbell is very cool," he'd told me.

"She is?"

"Yeah! She's really smart and opinionated," Kieron had explained thoughtfully. "Whenever we've had debates in class, she's won easy-peasy."

"So, she's one of the popular crowd," I'd said,

stunned by this observation. I'd only been hanging out with her for a day by this point, but I hadn't noticed her being surrounded by people clamouring to be friends with her and hanging on to her every word.

Plus, there was that whole falling-into-a-bin story.

"No, she's never seemed interested in being popular." Kieron had shrugged. "She likes to do her own thing and tends to keep herself to herself unless she's speaking up about something – I've always been a bit too intimidated to talk to her, to be honest."

"Wow." I'd bitten my lip. "I wonder why she'd want to be friends with me."

"You know, she saved one of the trees on the school grounds last year," he'd said, excited to fill me in. "They were going to chop it down to expand the car park, but she did all this research about the tree's history, and handed out leaflets to all the students and teachers about why the tree should be saved. She would stay late after school to stand by the tree with signs, protesting. In the end, Ms Sanderson listened to her and said the tree would be left alone. She even commissioned a little plaque to be made for it with the interesting information that Ivy had discovered – according to legend, an ancient knight of the realm once fought an evil sorcerer by that very tree. I actually wrote a piece about Ivy's protest for my blog."

"Seriously? Did you tell Ivy that?"

He'd shaken his head. "Nope."

"You should have done! I bet she'd feel honoured to have featured on your blog."

He'd snorted. "Hardly."

"Hey, you're a famous journalist now! You got the exclusive interview on the Super Animal Adventurers," I'd reminded him, making him laugh. "You should have more confidence in yourself."

"We both should," he'd replied. "It doesn't surprise me at all that someone as cool as Ivy Campbell would want to be friends with you. And it shouldn't surprise you, either."

The next day at school, I'd invited Ivy to sit with

us at lunch. When Kieron gets nervous, he talks a LOT, and he'd bombarded her with questions whilst also informing her of his journalistic ambitions. She'd wrinkled her nose at his admission.

"I don't really like journalists," she'd said, much to Kieron's horror.

"Why would you say that?" he'd asked, aghast.

"I don't like how they spin facts to suit their agenda," she'd replied matter-of-factly. "They feed people their opinions but present it as the truth. It's sly and manipulative."

"Ah." Kieron had nodded, smiling at her as though it suddenly made sense. "Then you don't like *irresponsible* journalists. That's absolutely fine, because I'm not one of those. I'm a good one."

She'd laughed in surprise at his answer. After that, she became as talkative as him – between the two of them, I could hardly get a word in edgeways – and since then, the three of us have stuck together at school. I wish I could have spent more time with them both outside of it, but I've been too busy with rescue missions to have any evenings to myself, and last weekend I spent the whole of Saturday helping to save hostages in a bank robbery. As the burglar was brought out in handcuffs to the cheer of the crowd who'd gathered to watch it all play out, he'd asked if he could have a quick selfie with me and the animals.

It was surreal.

"Guests will be arriving at any moment," Nan says on the day of the lunch, her head buried in the cupboard as she looks for a salad bowl. "Luna, please can you get out the serving spoons?"

I nod, opening the cutlery drawer, while Dad battles with the tablecloths outside in the garden. Nan is insisting on hosting the day outside despite the weather turning autumnal. It is sunny, just a little colder and windier as we get into late September.

"Where is Blizzard?" Nan demands to know, plonking the salad bowl on the kitchen table. "If I find him anywhere near this spread of food…"

"He's in my bedroom," I assure her, glancing out through the window where I see Stripes and Talon both sitting on the garden wall watching Dad in great amusement as he gets stuck in the tablecloths. Silver is in his bed in the kitchen keeping an eye on me and Nan, and I'm not sure where Chomp is.

"Shut away in your bedroom, I hope," Nan checks.

"I've told him that he'll only be allowed out if he behaves himself and if he's under my complete supervision. But he wanted to take a nap on my pillow anyway," I say, passing her the serving spoons so she can toss the salad. "He seems very tired today."

"I'm not surprised. I'm glad you had a bit of a lie-in this morning, too," Nan says, pausing for a moment to put her hands on her hips and give me a stern look. "Are you sure you haven't taken on too much, Luna?"

"What do you mean?"

"You're trying to juggle school with these rescue missions that the police send you on – when are you finding time to do your homework?" she questions.

"I told you, the teachers are being lenient with me. They've all given me extensions."

"Those extensions won't last forever. I'm not sure when you expect to get this work done that must be piling up. You haven't had a night off this week!"

"I had Thursday night off," I point out.

"Yes, and you spent it down at Lucy's rescue centre with Kieron, picking out fleas."

"I wasn't picking out fleas, Nan!" I giggle. "I was helping to bathe the dogs. It's fun!"

She reaches out to cup my face in her hands. "I worry about you, Luna. You're always so busy; rushing around the place; no time for fun. Barely any time to breathe. All this super-animal business…" She sighs. "I understand that the magic chose you to help them transform, but you're still so young. I'm not sure your mum meant for you to have such responsibility at this age."

"Nan, I'm *fine*, I promise," I insist, giving her the most convincing smile I can muster. "You know that I love being with the animals."

"I know, I know." She straightens and returns her attention to her salad. "As long as you know that you can always talk to me if ever it's feeling a bit too much. I can talk to Chief Superintendent Reece. And if you need help relaxing, you can always join me for my meditation classes."

"Thanks, Nan."

"Mind you take care of yourself," she says, waggling a finger at me. "It's important to rest. You know your great-great-grandfather stretched himself very thin by deciding to take up tightrope walking around his job. He insisted on training with the local circus every night when his wife begged him to rest. You know what happened to him?"

I try to suppress a smile, all too aware of Nan's tendency to tell outrageous stories that she claims are true.

"What?"

"His heart gave out when he was mid-air on the rope. He fell several metres and very nearly died, but luckily there happened to be a doctor in the tent that day, having operated on a fire-eater's throat just a few minutes earlier. He saved his life and demanded that he *rest* – he told him that next time, he might not be so lucky."

"Are you sure his heart didn't give out because he was so high off the ground on the tightrope?" I suggest, trying to sneak a salt-fish fritter from a plate and getting my hand quickly slapped away.

"No, young lady, that was not the reason," she says, narrowing her eyes at me. "He was perfectly used to heights. It was because he worked non-stop. Now, will you *please* go outside to help Richard with that tablecloth because I cannot watch him dance around inside of it any more."

I follow her instruction and rush to rescue Dad, who is grappling with the cloth over his face, about to walk slap bang into a tree. Stripes lets out a sniggering hiss as I stop him just in time and Silver, who has followed me out, gives her a sharp glare.

In just a few minutes, people come trickling through the kitchen out into the garden and I quickly tell the animals to be on their best behaviour before turning to greet my aunts, uncles and cousins, all of whom are desperate to hear how I'm getting on at school. Blushing under the attention, I'm pleased when Nan calls me away from them because the doorbell has gone again and she's taking a dish out the oven.

Gladly escaping from the chaos of the garden, I rush through the house to swing open the front door and find Ivy waiting on our doorstep, holding a tray of brownies.

"Hey!" I beam at her, standing aside to let her in.

"Hi, Luna, thanks again for inviting me," she says, passing me the brownies. "I baked these this morning, but I'm not sure if they're any good. I've never really baked before."

"Thanks! Come on through."

I lead her into the kitchen, where Nan spots her and, breaking into a wide smile, she potters over and envelops her in a large hug.

"You must be Ivy," Nan says warmly. "I'm Clementine, Luna's nan."

"Ivy made brownies today," I say, placing the tray carefully on the table.

"How wonderful," Nan says, admiring them. "Thank you."

"I was saying to Luna, though, this was my first attempt at baking, so they're probably terrible," she blurts out quickly. "I had to cut off the edges, they were burnt."

"They look delicious," Nan assures her sincerely. "Baking is all about having fun, and trial and error is very much a part of it. It took me years before I perfected my fruit cake and even now I can get it wrong. Did your dad teach you how to bake?"

Ivy snorts at the idea. "No, I got this recipe from online."

"Your dad isn't much of a cook then, I take it," Nan says, chuckling at her reaction.

"No, he eats out a lot. All the time, really," she tells us, looking down at the ground, her cheeks flushing.

"Well, I'm sure these brownies will be great," Nan emphasizes, beaming at her. "If you enjoyed your baking this morning, I'd be delighted to teach you some of my own recipes. You're welcome here any time."

Ivy brightens. "Really?"

"Absolutely!" Nan exclaims. "It would be an honour to have a keen student for once. Last time I tried to teach Luna one of our family recipes, I caught her sneaking most of it to the dog."

"It's a compliment! You know how much Silver enjoys your cooking, Nan," I say, sharing a mischievous smile with Ivy.

"Uh-huh." Nan rolls her eyes. "Right, you two, why don't you bring your brownies outside and go join the party? Everyone is excited to meet you, Ivy. Off you go, Luna, you lead the way and look after our guest."

"Will do," I say, stopping briefly to offer Ivy a quiet warning. "As I mentioned at school, there are a lot of people here and I find my family can be a little overbearing, so if they ask too many questions and it's all getting a bit much, please just say and we can go. It was really nice of you to come. I don't want you to feel—"

"Luna," she interrupts, "there is no chance that I'll want to leave anytime soon."

"I don't know, you've only just arrived," I point

out, as everyone turns to look in our direction. "These sorts of situations make me feel nervous, so I'll understand if it's too overwhelming. You'd probably want to spend your weekend doing something else."

"What could be better than spending a weekend surrounded by family? You're so lucky, Luna." She steps confidently past me, holding out the tray and giving everyone a winning smile. "Would anyone like a homemade brownie?"

Not only is Ivy a big hit with my family, but she quickly becomes adored by the animals, too. As soon as Silver came over to her, she crouched down to greet him, winning him over with a good neck scratch and a belly rub, receiving a slobbery lick across the face in return. She admired Talon, who was keeping her distance up in the beautiful bird house that Nan's choir friend, Marjorie, hand carved for her, and she made the time to go visit Blizzard up in my bedroom. She played with

Chomp in a pile of leaves, and Stripes – who can be stand-offish, especially with strangers – took to her instantly.

"Now that I think about it, Stripes and Ivy are quite similar characters," Kieron muses at one point, watching Stripes trot along next to Ivy as she approaches the food table to help herself to more of Nan's fruit cake. "Smart, determined, slightly aloof, and I wouldn't want to mess with either of them."

Later that afternoon, I'm listening to Uncle Desmond tell the story of the time he got chased by a bull in Devon, when I'm distracted by Dad looking horrified by a notification that pings on his phone. Politely excusing me from the conversation, Dad asks me to follow him inside, Silver trotting alongside us.

"What's going on?" I ask, checking I have the radio on me in case the police make a call. "Has something happened?"

"We need to turn on the news," he replies, leading

95

me into the sitting room and searching for the TV remote. A serious-looking newsreader flashes up on the screen, reading out the latest headline.

"And back to the breaking news of today: super animals have been completely out of control in the middle of London's Trafalgar Square," she announces.

Dad looks at me, panicked. I inhale sharply.

"What's going on?" Kieron asks, rushing into the room, accompanied by Lucy, Ivy and Nan. "I got a news notification about the super animals getting loose?"

"That's impossible!" Lucy exclaims. "They're right here with us."

"What's she saying?" Nan asks, gesturing to the news anchor. "Richard, turn it up, please."

He does so and we all gather round the screen to listen intently.

"A total of three super animals were seen this morning by hundreds of witnesses tearing around central London," the anchor reports. "After creating a scene of chaos and widespread panic, the animals disappeared quite suddenly, leaving no hints as to their current whereabouts. Glen Philips reports live now from Trafalgar Square. Over to you, Glen."

Trafalgar Square is shown taped off and empty, while serious-looking police officers patrol the area. Standing in front of the camera, the reporter lifts his microphone and gestures to the scene behind him.

"Thank you, Emma. Yes, as you can see behind me, Trafalgar Square, which is usually buzzing with tourists and Londoners, is now deserted, the pavements littered with items abandoned as people ran for their lives. This morning, witnesses describe three small pets transforming into what has become known as 'super animals' – a cheetah, a rhinoceros and an elephant began trampling through the square, leaving chaos in their wake. It is believed the elephant jumped into one of the fountains, filled his trunk and

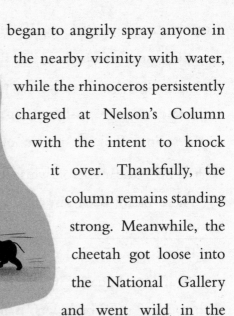

began to angrily spray anyone in the nearby vicinity with water, while the rhinoceros persistently charged at Nelson's Column with the intent to knock it over. Thankfully, the column remains standing strong. Meanwhile, the cheetah got loose into the National Gallery and went wild in the gift shop, scattering postcards, keyrings, mugs and rubber-tipped pencils everywhere. There have been reports that she had the priceless paintings in her sights, but luckily, she was rounded up before she could get her claws into those."

I watch the report in disbelief. Dad reaches out to place a hand on my shoulder.

"Glen, we can see the huge police presence there behind you," the anchor says from behind the desk, cutting in to ask a question. "Is there any word on who could be behind this vicious and unprovoked attack?"

"Oh no," I hear Kieron whisper.

"There hasn't been any confirmation as yet on who set these so-called 'super animals' loose," Glen replies into his mic, "however, it is safe to say that the key suspect will be Luna Wolf – the only person known to be in possession of these kind of creatures and with the ability to control them."

I feel like my breath has been knocked out of my body.

"Now, we do know that Luna Wolf has been working with the emergency services recently," Glen continues, "but there are those who have been sceptical of Chief Superintendent Reece's decision to bring Luna Wolf on board; those who believe it is dangerous to work alongside these potentially violent animals. Those sceptics will surely be using today as a key example of how bad it can be when Luna Wolf loses control."

Lucy lets out a gasp of indignation. "He can't be serious!"

"This is not good," Ivy mutters.

"Thank you, Glen," the anchor says, as we return to her in the studio. "We'll be bringing you more on that story as soon as we can. The lead news story once again there for you: super animals rampage through central London, leaving destruction in their wake. This prompts us to ask ourselves the question," she says, looking directly into the camera, "can Luna Wolf really be trusted?"

CHAPTER SIX

I thought it was bad when people at school were staring at me because I was famous for doing something good, but it's much worse being the centre of attention when everyone thinks you've done something bad. The moment I enter a room, it falls silent and I can feel people's eyes boring into my back as I walk along the corridors. I can tell that some students are nervous around me, or even scared – one boy literally yelped and jumped out of my way when I asked if I could get by.

"Ignore them," Ivy says one lunch break, purposefully raising her voice so people around us can hear. "If they believe any of that rubbish about you and those out-of-control animals, then they're idiots."

"Exactly," Kieron agrees loudly, narrowing his eyes at the cluster of people on the table next to us who are openly staring. "Anyone with a brain can tell you're innocent."

There's a momentary pause followed by a chorus of clattering trays as the group quickly stands up and moves tables to the other side of the canteen.

The whole room is watching in silence.

I overhear a whisper from a girl nearby: "Why do they even let her come to school?"

"I know," her friend hisses. "She's putting all of us in danger."

Hot tears prick at my eyes, threatening to spill over. Swallowing the lump in my throat, I push back my chair and stand up, grabbing my tray.

"Wait, Luna, where are you going?" Ivy asks, worried.

"Outside," I mutter, shuffling towards the door with my head bowed.

"Good idea," Ivy replies, hurriedly getting to her feet.

"Yes, I much prefer eating *al fresco*," Kieron declares, marching out behind me.

Heading out of the main building into the yard by the sports fields, I find a deserted picnic bench and plonk my tray of food down on to it, even though I'm too upset to eat. It's a grey, drizzly day and it's cold in the wind, but Kieron and Ivy loyally place their trays next to mine before Kieron runs back in to fetch our coats from our lockers.

"This is much better than sitting inside that stuffy canteen," he says as he returns. "It's very refreshing out here."

I can't help but smile at his determination to remain upbeat. It's been difficult to remain positive since what happened at Trafalgar Square – those animals haven't been found and no one knows where they came from, so it's not exactly surprising that so many people think I have something to do with it.

I've released a statement saying I'm innocent, but it

was ignored by the media. Instead, most publications have chosen to focus on what all of my outspoken critics say about me. Chief Superintendent Reece has done her best to calm the public by reassuring them that there has been no evidence to suggest that those three animals were in any way linked to me, but since there are no other suspects, her support hasn't done much.

"After all you've done on those rescue missions, this is how you're thanked." Nan tutted when a debate over whether I should be allowed to help the police was aired on TV. She quickly switched it off before turning to me and sternly saying, "*You* know who you are, Luna. That's all that matters."

Which is all very well, but it's hard to remember that when so many people are publicly saying that I'm a "menace to society".

Nan's house remains surrounded by paparazzi – poor Dad is being hounded by reporters every time he leaves the house to go to work. Nan has insisted on skipping all of her various classes to be at home with me in the evenings, and Lucy and Kieron have had to stay away so they don't get caught up in it. The animals are all cooped up and for the last few days, we haven't been asked to help the emergency services for any rescues – Chief Superintendent Reece thinks it's best if I lie low for a while.

The only thing that brings any joy to the house is how Nan waits for a reporter to unwittingly position themselves in the wrong place on the lawn and then she quickly turns on the sprinklers, cackling with laughter as they get soaked.

I wish I didn't have to come to school, but Dad has said that he thinks it's a good distraction. He's wrong – it's all that anyone at school can talk about.

"Thanks for joining me out here," I say to Kieron and Ivy, feeling guilty for dragging them out of the canteen. "I'm so sorry about everything that's happened."

"You have nothing to apologize for," Ivy strongly insists, her eyebrows furrowed crossly. "It's not your fault."

"Everyone thinks I'm guilty," I say glumly.

"No, they don't. That's what the media want

you to believe – they trick you into making you think a certain way," Ivy says, rolling her eyes. "The headlines about you will die down soon enough. Next week there will be a new story and everyone will move on."

"I hope so," I say, but I'm not convinced. "Everywhere I go I feel like I'm not wanted. Like I put everyone on edge. People out there think me and the animals belong behind bars."

"No one thinks that!" Kieron protests.

I get out my phone and show him one of today's tabloid headlines: "MP DECLARES THAT LUNA WOLF AND HER SUPER ANIMALS 'BELONG BEHIND BARS'".

"That's one person and he only said it to get attention," Kieron assures me.

"His quotes about me are everywhere I look. According to him, my 'dangerous" animals should be taken away by the authorities and I should be arrested for disorderly conduct."

"You shouldn't be reading any of those articles,"

Ivy advises. "They just care about clicks and views; that's why they publish the most outrageous statements possible, regardless of the integrity involved."

"Ivy's right," Kieron assures me gently. "The people that matter know that all of these articles are made up of rumours and conjecture. We know the truth and that's what counts."

I sigh, wondering how much trouble I'd get into if I skipped the rest of school today and went home to hide away and cuddle Silver. Even though I'm away from him during the day, I still feel our strong connection and I know that he's waiting for me to come home.

As Lucy always says, no matter how bad it gets, dogs make everything better.

"I wish we knew the *whole* truth, though," Kieron adds thoughtfully.

Ivy tilts her head at him. "What do you mean?"

"Who owns those animals? How are those three animals even in existence?" he questions curiously.

"We know from our research into Luna's mum's work that Magnitude was a project with just five prototypes: Silver, Stripes, Blizzard, Chomp and Talon. She rescued those five animals and destroyed the magical source except for the pendant that Luna is wearing right now."

"Did anyone have the necklace before you, Luna?" Ivy asks.

I shake my head. "It was given to me when Mum died. And both Kieron and I witnessed the fact that it doesn't work for anyone but me anyway."

"Are you sure that Magnitude only had five animals?" Ivy checks.

"Yes. We're certain," Kieron confirms.

Ivy frowns. "So how is it possible that there are three unaccounted for?"

"It doesn't make sense," I say, resting my chin in my hands. "Kieron, when Rex Robinson sent you all the work he'd put together about Magnitude, did he mention any competitors? Any other companies running similar projects?"

"No. There was nothing about that."

"So, where do you think these animals have come from?" Ivy asks. "Is there any way that Magnitude could secretly be up and running again?"

My blood runs cold at the thought.

"It's possible. They never caught the person behind Magnitude," Kieron reasons. "The police arrested Dr Callahan and the people working for him, but there was someone else. Someone more powerful than Callahan who was financing the Magnitude project."

"But how could Magnitude be back in motion?" I ask Kieron desperately. "I have the magic! It's not possible for the animals to transform without it."

"We don't know that your mum destroyed *all* of the magic," Kieron says, his brow furrowed.

"Yes, we do. Rex Robinson said she did."

"What if there is more of the magical source out there that your mum didn't know about?" Kieron says. "I'll contact Rex and ask him if Athena ever talked about where the magic source was found and if there could be anyone else who had some in their possession. Or maybe Callahan and his Magnitude colleagues have managed to get their hands on some more."

"Dr Callahan is in prison, isn't he?" Ivy checks.

"That's right," I confirm. "Plus, the magic didn't work for him even when he did have the necklace."

"Was there anyone else who could wield the magic?" Ivy asks.

"No one but Athena Wolf, Luna's mum," Kieron says proudly, shooting me a smile. "She was the only scientist who was good enough to work on it. Callahan was always in her shadow – he never came close to being worthy."

"What about the other scientists who worked on Magnitude?" Ivy asks. "Is there a way of finding out who else worked with your mum, Luna?"

"Not easily," Kieron answers as I shrug. "Last time, almost everything I discovered about Magnitude came from the unpublished article by Rex Robinson."

"And he got his information from Mum," I

add for Ivy's benefit. "Magnitude made sure that their tracks were covered when the project was abandoned."

Kieron sighs, rubbing his forehead thoughtfully. "But I do think you're right, Ivy – looking for former Magnitude employees might lead us to the person who is controlling these new super animals. There must be more of the magical source than we thought, and chances are that someone in Magnitude was in the know."

"You've just said that it would be impossible to track them down."

"I said it wouldn't be easy, not impossible," he corrects, a mischievous glint in his eye. "Sometimes, my dedication to the work means that I attempt to access systems that are closed off to the general public, so that I can find information that certain organizations are attempting to hide or cover up."

Ivy stares at him. "Are you talking about hacking?"

"I'm talking about uncovering information that should be public," he says tactfully.

"So you're the kind of journalist who exposes powerful corporations and the people who run them," she says.

He presses his lips together. "Look, I know you hate journalists and probably think that it's bad to—"

"Actually, I think that's really brave of you," Ivy interrupts. Her eyes fall to the floor as she adds quietly, "If you know people are doing something wrong, it's important to do what you can to stop them."

Kieron looks a little taken aback, before grinning at her, his cheeks flushing.

"Exactly," he says. "So, after school today I'll start doing some digging around Magnitude and we'll see how far I get."

"Kieron, I don't want you getting involved," I insist stubbornly. "Remember what happened last time you did some 'digging" into Magnitude? Your mum was kidnapped!"

"Yeah, and it was fine in the end. You saved her," he says, before adding to Ivy, "And I took out a guy using a tennis-ball blaster. I'll tell you all about it later."

"But, Kieron, whoever is behind these new super animals could be really dangerous," I say. "They've already set them loose in London without caring about the consequences. Who knows how they'll react if they find out you are trying to track them down? I really don't want anyone getting hurt."

"Luna, someone has to find out the truth," Kieron declares, puffing out his chest. "And I think that someone should be me."

I can't help but smile at him. "OK. Thanks, Kieron."

"Glad to be of assistance to the Animal Wizard once again," he says, giving me a noble salute.

"Just be careful," I warn him, "because who knows who's behind these animals and what they're planning next?"

Later that day, somewhere a few miles
north of London...

A shrill creak pierces the silence of the night as Dr Callahan tentatively pushes through a turnstile.

He winces at the sound, holding up the torch light on his phone and shining it out in front of him. He can make out a small hut with its windows boarded up to the left of the pathway, with a sign reading "INFORMATION" across the top of it, but beyond that, straight ahead, is a huge glass domed building. Callahan gasps at the magnificent structure, before jumping in fright at the shadows within it. Realizing quickly that the silhouettes inside are tall plants and not people, he breathes a sigh of relief, placing a hand on his chest.

"What is this place?" he asks out loud with an involuntary shudder.

Once again checking the text message he received earlier today, he confirms he's definitely at the right address. The location is not too far north of London, but somehow it feels like he's ventured deep into the countryside. There's nothing else for miles, just an empty stretch of land with this strange glass building constructed in the middle of it.

Callahan wonders if he's supposed to go into the glasshouse or wait outside of it. The message didn't give any further information beyond the time and place he had to meet.

"H-hello?" he calls out into the darkness.

"BOO!" a voice barks back, making him squeal in terror.

When Callahan hears the tittering that follows his reaction, his fear quickly turns to irritation.

"*Chad*. It's you," he mutters as his former criminal associate comes out from behind the information kiosk. "I assume that if you're here, Dean can't be far behind."

"You should have seen your face," Dean remarks, confirming Callahan's suspicions as he appears next to Chad, shining the torch light on his phone into Callahan's eyes. "You were terrified!"

Callahan squints in the light, disappointed that his boss clearly went to the trouble of getting Dean and

Chad released from prison early, too. Having worked with them both in the lead-up to his incarceration, Callahan can safely say that they hardly share a brain cell between them.

"I was *not* terrified," Callahan insists pompously, running a hand through his curly mop of hair.

Dean snorts. "Then why did you scream so loud?"

"I shouldn't think it's that uncommon for people to scream when they realize that *you're* nearby, Dean," Callahan says with a lingering sneer.

Dean's eyes flash with anger. "You—"

"What are you doing here, Callahan?" Chad interrupts before Dean can do anything stupid.

"The Boss asked me to come."

Chad rubs his chin. "That's interesting. I'm surprised he still trusts you, after everything that happened with Luna Wolf. You didn't get all the prototype animals back and she got away with the magical source. A *complete* failure of your mission, you could say."

Callahan bristles. "I seem to remember that it was all three of us who failed him."

"*You* hired us, remember?" Chad points out. "I'm just glad that the Boss saw our potential during the whole fiasco and allowed us to join his team officially. You're not in charge of us any more, Callahan. We're equals now."

"Don't flatter yourself," Callahan hisses. "I'm a leading Magnitude scientist. You're nothing more than … bumbling fools!"

"Hey! I do not bumble!" Dean huffs.

Callahan smirks. "But you agree you are a fool?"

"Now, just you wait a second, you're twisting things," Dean says, narrowing his eyes.

"And just when I thought you couldn't be even more pathetic, I heard you blabbed the whole story to the police," Callahan concludes, tutting. "How embarrassing, Dean. I may have failed in our mission, but at least I'm not a snitch."

"You've gone too far," Dean bellows, rolling up his sleeves and rounding on Callahan. "I will—"

A cold, chilling voice interrupts: "Gentlemen."

Dean instantly stops, dropping his fists and bowing his head, stepping back from Callahan. Chad and Callahan stand to attention. A tall, broad man dressed in an expensive tailored suit has quietly approached them and is watching their interaction with intrigue.

"Let's keep this friendly, shall we?" he says simply, the calm authority in his voice causing Callahan to give an involuntary shudder.

"Of course, sir," Callahan says meekly.

"It is no secret that you disappointed me greatly last time you worked together, but I didn't use my contacts to get the three of you out of prison early just so you could brawl," the suited man states. "We have work to do and I don't have time for your personal vendettas. Is that clear?"

"Crystal," Callahan replies without hesitation.

Chad nods and Dean gives a reluctant grunt, glaring at Callahan all the while.

"Good, let's go, then."

The three of them follow him into the dome building, walking down a main path that's been designed to weave through the glasshouse from one side to the other. Surrounding the path are plants of every shape, size and colour, many of them towering over Callahan as he scurries after his boss, looking up at them in awe.

"Sir, where are we?" he asks in a whisper, as they pass through a small round clearing in the very centre of the dome, in which sits a hand-carved circular bench, designed for visitors to take a pause if needed.

"It's like strolling through a mini jungle," Chad remarks, looking up at the stars visible through the curved ceiling.

"It was going to be my botanical gardens," their boss answers wistfully. "I had great plans for it when I bought it years ago. I thought it could make me a lot of money – but I got distracted by Magnitude and never got round to finishing this project. Anyway, it's proved useful – it's a big enough space for secret scientific experimentation. At some point I'll knock this down and turn it into luxury flats. Pity about the gardens though. I was going to name the complex after myself."

"The Hunter Botanical Gardens," Callahan says. "I like it!"

"Don't be ridiculous, Callahan. I wasn't going to use my first name. I would use my surname," Hunter corrects, causing Callahan to blush. "That's my brand, after all."

"This place gives me the creeps," Dean says gruffly behind Callahan, swatting a large protruding leaf out of his way. "I don't like nature."

"Some of these exotic plants are man-eating ones, too," Chad tells him.

Dean gasps, jumping away from a particularly spiky one that he's passing. Chad sniggers and Dean glares at him.

Hunter clears his throat pointedly and they fall into silence.

As they reach the back of the dome, Hunter leads the group outside. In the middle of the land that stretches out in front of them is a large square area that has been fenced off. Callahan notes that while the rest of the complex feels fairly neglected, this tall metal fencing outside looks newly constructed. Hunter opens a small silver security box that's attached to the fence, pressing a red button inside, and a series of industrial floodlights lining the perimeter of the square turn on, bathing the grass in a bright white light.

Someone opens the gate at the opposite end of the area and sets down what looks like two small boxes balancing on a cat box. Callahan tries to make out who it is, but the lights are too bright and all he can see is a figure unlocking the carrier and encouraging the creature within to exit by rapping on the side of the box with their knuckles.

A Bengal cat eventually jumps out, looking about

the yard warily, her bright green eyes glinting in the artificial light. The next box is then opened, from which a tiny mouse darts out, scurrying busily across the grass. A hedgehog is released from the final box, rolled out by the mysterious person who quickly exits again, locking the door securely behind them.

"I trust you all enjoyed the performance of our animals in Trafalgar Square," Hunter prompts, clasping his hands behind his back.

"I didn't think it was possible when you told me on that prison visit that you had more super animals in the works," Callahan admits. "But I saw the footage. It's incredible!"

"Did you see everyone scarpering?" Dean snorts, chuckling to himself. "They were all so scared. Hilarious. I watched it on social media several times." He points at the animals beyond the fencing. "Is that them?"

Instead of answering, Hunter responds with a knowing smile.

Suddenly, there's a flash of bright blue light.

Where the Bengal cat was sitting is now a tall, slender cheetah, her tail swishing side to side; where the hedgehog was curled up, frightened and still, now stands a large rhinoceros; and instead of a mouse dashing about nervously, there's a gigantic elephant, lifting its trunk to emit a loud, echoing trumpet sound.

Callahan smiles in amazement.

"How did you—"

He is interrupted by the thundering noise of the elephant furiously stomping around the grass as though agitated, his trunk swinging wildly as he tears through the space. He narrowly misses flattening the cheetah, who jumps out of his way just in time. Letting out an explosive yelp in distress, the cheetah's eyes quickly grow fierce; she ducks her head low to the ground and hisses and growls threateningly to the men beyond the fence, opening her jaws to reveal her razor-sharp fangs, the fur down her back sticking up on end. Rattled and confused, the rhinoceros joins in the sudden frenzy, grunting and squealing as she paws at the ground impatiently.

As the elephant continues to stomp around uncontrollably, the cheetah pounces at the fence, clawing up it frantically before launching herself off and racing across the ground in a blur to bounce off the opposite fence. Meanwhile, the rhinoceros spots Hunter and the group of men with him. Her eyes flashing with fury and letting out a snort, she bows her head and pelts towards them at full speed with a raging cry.

Dean squeaks. Chad inhales sharply. Callahan cowers.

Hunter doesn't flinch.

The yard is consumed by another flash of light and when Callahan lowers the arm shielding his face, there is no rhino stampeding angrily towards him but the curled spiky ball of a little hedgehog rolling along the ground, coming to a stop as she hits the fence. Behind the hedgehog, the cheetah has returned to her form of a Bengal cat, hissing and spitting as she backs herself into a corner, bewildered.

No longer an elephant, the mouse sits up against the fence, his whiskers trembling.

"Callahan, these animals are my prized possessions," Hunter states coldly, turning to him with a determined glint in his eye. "As you should know by now, I like everything I own to be perfect and controlled. These are far from that. If I'm going to be known around the world for having the largest collection of super creatures, then I need them to be in working order. Your job is to get back to the laboratory and iron out the kinks."

"I'm so pleased to be of service, sir," Callahan gushes, glancing nervously at the animals. "May I ask … how did you do this? Where did you get that magic? And who was that at the other end of the pen?"

"An old friend of yours, Callahan," Hunter informs him, relishing the mystery. "Before I reacquaint you with them, do I have your word that you'll get these animals under control? I don't have any more time or patience for further failure, so if you're not up to the challenge then I'll find a better scientist who is."

"None in existence, sir," Callahan says, trying to sound more confident than he feels. "I was always the best at Magnitude. That hasn't changed. I will somehow … er … fix them."

Hunter narrows his eyes at him.

"You'd better," he growls.

Callahan gulps.

"As for you two," Hunter continues, turning to Chad and Dean, "we've decided to capitalize on the chaos that these animals can provide. As we'd hoped, their antics have put Luna Wolf in a difficult position and with a few more 'incidents', shall we say, there will be great pressure on her to give up the five super animals currently under control. Once she does, we'll take them back. They belong in my collection, after all."

"Makes sense to me." Chad nods. "What do you need us to do?"

The corners of Hunter's mouth twist into a menacing smile.

"Take the animals and get creative," he instructs.

"Make sure it's public, so we get the most press possible. Luna Wolf has to become public enemy number one."

"How can we be sure that she'll get *bad* publicity?" Chad points out. "They might paint her as a hero. They did after that bridge rescue."

"You don't need to worry about that," Hunter assures him. "I have it on good authority that the media will play ball. They'll make her a baddie, they just need the right circumstances. That's up to you two, Chad and Dean."

"We won't let you down," Dean says excitedly. "We'll make sure those animals cause total carnage."

"Good. Remember, the more people, the more witnesses," Hunter concludes. "And the greater the danger, the better."

CHAPTER SEVEN

Walking into the party for the grand opening night of the newly discovered royal tiara is like stepping into whole other world where everything is sparkling and glittering, and everyone in it is impossibly beautiful and glamorous.

It's being held at Shakespeare's Globe Theatre on London's Southbank, where the tiara will be on display for a couple of weeks before becoming part of a permanent exhibition at the Tower of London. There's a long red carpet leading up to the door of the theatre and the rope lines are bursting with the paparazzi and crowds of excited fans, hoping to catch a glimpse of all the royal families and A-list celebrities attending tonight.

I thought no one would care about seeing me or, if they did, they'd be angry about the Trafalgar Square incident and throw tomatoes at me or something. Thankfully, I'm wrong. No one throws fruit at me. Instead, there are people shouting my name, calling me over, begging for selfies with me and the animals – all five of whom have been invited tonight, too. Stripes and Silver are both at my feet, Chomp and Blizzard are each perched on a shoulder, and Talon flits just above my head. I'm so glad that they're here with me, as well as Nan, because I would have been much too nervous to go to an event like this on my own.

Nan looks incredible. She's wearing a long orange dress with flowing sleeves and these huge gold statement earrings that jangle and catch the light whenever she moves her head. She bought the dress this week when she and Lucy insisted we all go on a shopping excursion together to pick out special

outfits for such a fancy occasion. It took visits to a few shops for me to decide what I was going to wear because I didn't really know what I was looking for, but as soon as I saw this dress, I knew it was perfect for one main reason.

"It's silver," Nan had observed with a knowing smile as I lifted its hanger from the rail and held the dress up to admire it.

"If you have a wolf, it makes sense to match him," Lucy had observed with a chuckle.

I'd told her I couldn't agree more.

When I put the dress on earlier this evening, pairing it with black tights and chunky black boots, I looked at myself in the mirror and smiled at my reflection. I've never dressed up like this before because I've never had reason to, and I felt special wearing such a cool dress. Dad had knocked on the door and when I'd told him to come in, he'd given me a huge beaming smile, pressing a hand to his heart.

"You look amazing, Luna," he'd said proudly.

I'd turned back to my reflection and reached to the necklace tucked safely behind the neckline of the dress.

"I miss her too," Dad had said, noticing my action. His eyes fell to the floor. "Your mum would have been very proud of you. And she'd have loved that dress."

Silver had barked in agreement from where he was lying on my bed.

Dad's comment had meant a lot. Shopping with Nan and Lucy had been so much fun and I was so grateful to both of them, but I'd found it a little difficult, too, because I knew that I was never going to have a special day out shopping for a big event with my own mum.

But I know I'm lucky to have Nan here with me tonight, and as the cameras all turn in our direction, I reach out to grab her hand, holding her tight. Silver can sense my nerves and he presses his weight against my leg to let me know that no matter what, he's right here with me. Although sprinting isn't usually one of my strong points, I fly down that red carpet so fast, dragging Nan behind me the whole way, that she tells me off as soon as I stop at the door where a man in a tux waits to hold it open for us.

"Do you want me to go over on my ankle and show my underpants to the world's press, Luna Wolf?" Nan huffs as I let go of her hand. "You almost broke my fingers, too! Didn't you want a nice photograph of you arriving with your fabulous nan and superstar animals? In the papers tomorrow, the picture of us will be a strange orange-and-silver blur!"

"Sorry, Nan," I say, glancing nervously at the glamorous pop star coming up the carpet behind us dutifully stopping to place a hand on her hip and give a smouldering look that's greeted with an eruption of camera flashes. "I didn't want to pose for the cameras. I would have felt stupid. I already feel like I don't belong here."

Nan's expression softens and she leans in towards me.

"Let me tell you a secret, Luna," she says conspiratorially. "No one feels completely at ease at events like this. Everyone here feels the pressure of being in the spotlight – it's not easy for anyone. And I can tell you, hand on heart, that you deserve to be here more than anyone. You need a night off after all those rescue missions. Come on, let's go in and see what all the fuss is about, shall we?"

Thanking the doorman, she leads me and the animals through into the theatre, where guests are gathered in the round yard space in the middle, chatting and laughing over the elegant music of a string quartet as they sip from dainty champagne flutes.

I've never been to the Globe before, but thanks

to Dad, who decided to treat Nan and me to a monologue all about the Globe's history yesterday over dinner, I know that it's been built to resemble the sixteenth-century timber-framed theatre where William Shakespeare's plays were first performed – the original Elizabethan building was destroyed in a fire. I'm gazing around the amphitheatre in awe, admiring the wooden seating tiers and striking columns, when my eyes fall on the roped-off pedestal in the middle of the stage. A black cushion sits on top of it, displaying the tiara, its pearls and gemstones glinting in its gold setting.

"No wonder people have come from all over the world to see it," Nan says to me.

"It's beautiful," I agree, before we're approached by a waiter offering us drinks.

Nan and I are happy to lurk by the back for a bit, keeping our distance and taking it all in, but we're soon spotted by Maximillian Fringe, a famous Hollywood actor, who rushes over to introduce himself and ask if the animals can transform there and then.

"I don't think that would be a good idea," Nan says politely.

"Shame!" he exclaims, his face falling with disappointment as he adjusts his silk neckerchief. "Has anyone told you that your story would make a great movie, Luna? It's got mystery, intrigue, magic and then a gripping disaster plot that no one saw coming! I have to say the Trafalgar Square pandemonium was a genius twist. Edge of your seat stuff!"

"No, that wasn't me or my animals, we don't actually know who—"

I'm interrupted by a woman onstage tapping a microphone to make sure it's working, and Maximillian tells me we'll chat later before disappearing into the crowd. Silver nudges my hand and I rest my palm on his head, taking a deep breath and trying to ignore the panic rising in my stomach as I notice people glancing warily in our direction. I wonder how many people in here think I'm dangerous.

Satisfied that the mic is working, the woman onstage welcomes us all and talks about the excitement of such a historic and priceless discovery. She encourages us to come and have a closer look at the tiara when we get the opportunity later in the evening. There's an enthusiastic round of applause as she concludes, and the music starts up again.

"Let's try to make our way to the front to see it properly," Nan suggests eagerly.

She begins to work out a path through the crowd, but she needn't have worried. As soon as people become aware of us nearby, they quickly move out of the way. Some seem keen to meet us; others are afraid. One woman looks down at Silver and lets out a dramatic gasp before shuffling as far back from him as possible. Stripes can't help but hiss at her.

Don't make things worse, I tell her with a sharp look.

She meows indignantly in response.

"We shouldn't have come," I whisper to Nan, who bristles at the suggestion. "Seriously, Nan, it's like it is at school. People believe what they read in the papers."

"Forget what everyone else may or may not be thinking, Luna," Nan encourages gently, offering anyone still staring a sharp look before stepping aside so I can get closer to the stage. She gestures to the tiara. "We're here to see this piece of history and we're very lucky to do so. Don't you agree? Now, I personally think that the tiara would look much better on my head than sitting on that cushion. Talon" – she looks up to address the sparrow, who has nestled happily in her hair – "you may have to make way for a crown."

I laugh and instantly feel better. Nan puts her arm around me, careful not to upset Chomp or Blizzard, and we stand together, admiring the tiara.

Suddenly, I notice Silver's ears prick up in alert.

He turns to look at the exit and whines.

Something's not right, he's saying.

The hair on Stripes's back stands on end and she begins to hiss loudly at the door.

A rock star standing close to us gives us a concerned look.

"What's up with your animals?" he asks.

"They... They look like they're about to transform!" shrieks the woman who was nervous around us earlier. "Luna Wolf's animals are going to transform!"

"No, no, they're not!" I say hurriedly, holding up my hands. "I think they can hear trouble in the distance, that's all. There's nothing to worry about!"

"They shouldn't be allowed at events like this if they can't be controlled," declares a well-known fashion designer, wrinkling her nose at the animals. She turns to the man standing over her shoulder and barks, "Terrence, get the car. I don't want to be anywhere around here when those creatures lose control."

"Everyone needs to remain calm," Nan insists with the kind of authority that people listen to. "As Luna has stated to the press, she had nothing to do with that unfortunate incident recently. There will be no out-of-control super animals here today."

At that exact moment, our attention is drawn to a darting movement up on the stage. A Bengal cat seems to appear out of nowhere. She stares right at me, her tail flicking from side to side. There's something about the way she's looking at me – I can't quite work it out, but it's as though she's trying to communicate with me.

I think she's scared, I tell Silver.

There's a blinding flash of blue light. It doesn't come from my necklace.

When it ebbs away, there's no longer a cat standing on the stage but a magnificent cheetah. Her eyes have changed – they're wild now, flashing with confusion and anger. She positions herself to pounce and bares her teeth.

The panic is instant. There's a chorus of screams as everyone turns on their heel to run towards the theatre exits as fast as they can, while trays of drinks and canapés go flying in the air as waiters make a dash for it alongside the guests.

"Luna!" Nan cries, helping up a pop star who

has fallen over in her towering heels while I remain where I was, transfixed by the cheetah. "You need to transform your animals!"

Before I have a chance to focus, the cheetah jumps up to the pedestal and clasps the tiara in her jaws, snatching it from its cushion and then disappearing through the curtains behind the stage.

"THIEF!" a security guard who's backed into a corner yells, pointing his finger at me.

I don't have time to protest my innocence because we hear a scream coming from the direction of the red carpet, nowhere near where the cheetah would have exited the theatre. Silver looks up at me.

There are more, he says.

I hesitate. If I transform my animals, people might think they're the ones causing the destruction. Helping could make everything worse.

We have to help. Trust us, Silver assures me, his golden eyes fixed on mine.

I know he's right. The animals prepare to transform while I gently pull the chain of my necklace out from under the neck of my dress and grip the pendant in my fingers. Shutting out the noise and chaos around me, I concentrate on the magic flowing within. A shimmering light, more powerful than the one that affected the Bengal cat, bathes the amphitheatre in a blue glow and when it dims, the super animals are ready to go.

I turn to Nan, who nods encouragingly at me.

"*Go*," she says.

We hear more screams. The animals and I spring into action, racing out of the theatre and emerging back on to the red carpet. The crowds have dispersed, belongings are strewn across the pavement, the ropes are knocked over on the ground and we soon understand why: a giant rhinoceros is stampeding up and down Bankside, mowing down anything in her path, sending chairs and tables outside restaurant flying as she lifts them with her horn and tosses them aside.

I notice a family taking cover underneath one table that will soon be right in the path of the

charging rhino. The parents look at the animal in horror, wrapping their arms tightly around their little girl crouched in between them.

Silver, go! I instruct, sending my wolf sprinting towards them.

He makes it just in time, halting in front of the cowering family and blocking the rhino's path. Standing strong, he bears his razor-sharp wolf teeth and lets out an almighty warning bark. The rhino sees him and skids to a sudden stop, shaking her head and snorting, her eyes flashing with fury. Silver lowers his head, ready to pounce, growling at her, and the family take the opportunity to escape their hiding place and run to safety.

"Thank you, Mr Wolf!" the girl cries over her dad's shoulder as he carries her away.

As the rhino hesitates, working out whether or not to charge, I notice a collar round her neck with a little black box attached to it. The box suddenly flashes red and she howls in pain. It jolts her to run again, but, put off by the wolf, she changes direction, rushing straight towards the river where two teenagers have stopped to film her on their phones. One ducks to the ground in fright, while the other screams and turns to climb the fence, before jumping into the river Thames.

Stripes, protect them, I communicate, sending my tiger quickly in their direction.

I turn to Chomp. *I need you in the water.*

As Chomp crawls towards the river, Stripes bounds over to place herself between the rhino and the teenager, roaring loudly. The rhino tries to stop in time but is running too fast – Stripes anticipates this and rather than waiting to take the impact of the rhino crashing into her, she pounces forwards to tackle her, sending them both rolling to the side. The teenager clambers to his feet and runs away, while his friend is saved from the water by Chomp.

With everything going on, I hadn't noticed the police force, who have now arrived on the scene and are moving towards us wearing their stab vests in a slow, cautious line.

"Bring your animals under control and put your hands up," one of them demands through a megaphone.

"Can't you see that her animals are saving everyone?" cries out Nan, who has emerged from Shakespeare's Globe holding a sword. She clocks my expression and rolls her eyes. "Don't worry, Luna, it's a prop sword that I found backstage. I could still do some damage with it if I needed to, I reckon."

"Please stay back there, Nan," I instruct, as she swishes the sword menacingly through the air.

The rhino has managed to get to her feet after the tiger tackle and is now looking at the line of police approaching her. She paws at the ground threateningly.

"Oh no," I whisper, before raising my voice to shout out to the police, "Stay back!"

As she begins her charge towards the police, they quickly realize that there's very little they can do to stop a furious rhinoceros and share glances of horror.

"TAKE COVER!" the officer with the megaphone bellows, throwing himself behind a bin and covering his head with his hands.

Stripes, slow her down but don't hurt her! I instruct my tiger, before searching for Silver and finding him waiting near the row of restaurants, his eyes flashing at me. *Silver, help Stripes.*

Hurtling at the speeding rhino, Stripes leaps into the air and manages to jump on the rhino's back, surprising her and bringing her to a stop, while Silver rushes over to position himself in front of the police officers and stop her from getting any closer. Having shaken Stripes off, the rhino glances from Silver to Stripes and back to Silver again as they pressure her to shuffle back towards the restaurant.

A high-pitched whistle from Talon pierces the air and I look up to see her hovering above the river, vying for my attention. She nods her head towards the Millennium Bridge.

My jaw drops.

The bridge is shaking under the weight of a huge elephant, who is stomping and crashing his way back and forth across it. Pedestrians are screaming as they run as fast as they can to safety on either side of it, while he threatens to bring the whole structure crashing down.

There's a loud whirring sound above us as a police helicopter flies overhead towards the elephant, lowering some kind of net. The elephant spots it and thunders to the edge of the bridge, stomping his feet even harder, shaking his head in a storm of rage. He dips his trunk into the Thames and then lifts it up high, pointing it straight at the helicopter before spraying it with a powerful stream of water. Struck by the force, the helicopter loses balance and I hear Nan squeal in fright as we watch the helicopter spin through the air. After a sickening wobble, it thankfully regains control and speeds away into the distance. Another helicopter has appeared to join the effort, but having seen what's just happened, sensibly turns round and flies away, too.

Trumpeting victoriously, the elephant returns to crushing as much as possible beneath his feet on his way back on to the bridge as though intent on bringing it down.

"You have to do something, Luna," Nan cries,

watching as the police evacuate the area while they wait for some form of backup. "It's up to you now!"

Talon, distract her, I communicate, giving my eagle a nod.

Talon pelts through the air towards the elephant, dipping to fly in a low circle around her head and get her attention.

Meanwhile, I turn to Blizzard, who has been waiting to help.

We need the strength of a polar bear, I tell him.

With a rumbling growl, he runs in the direction of the bridge.

Chomp, help him, I instruct as my crocodile appears on the bank's edge, having safely escorted the teenager back to shore and helped anyone else who attempted to swim across the Thames in an effort to escape the chaos.

Chomp propels himself towards the Millennium Bridge, hauling himself up the steps to follow Blizzard as the polar bear approaches the elephant. Talon has successfully captured the elephant's attention, circling her head and irritating her enough to try to catch the eagle in her trunk to no avail. Dizzy from chasing Talon round and round, the elephant trumpets angrily as she wobbles on her feet, before realizing there's a roaring polar bear thundering towards her. Blizzard slows as he gets closer, letting her find her footing. Regaining balance, she eyes the polar bear suspiciously and then glances over her shoulder to see Chomp lying in wait behind her, his jaws wide open. She turns back to face Blizzard, who goes up on his hind legs, as though warning her that he has the power to stop her should she choose to carry on.

I wait, my breath in my throat, as they square up to each other.

After a few moments, Blizzard turns his head to look all the way back at me. There may be a bit of a distance between us, but I can hear him in my head loud and clear.

She's frightened, he's telling me.

When he lowers himself down again to communicate that he's not going to hurt her, she responds by lowering her head as though in defeat. Even from here, I can see that she's tired and confused. She wants to stop.

A red light appears on the collar round the elephant's neck and she squeals, before beginning to stomp angrily again. Surprised by her sudden change in behaviour, Blizzard prepares to pounce. Before he can, though, the air is filled with a rumbling whirring sound and I look up to see a fleet of official helicopters flying in. They're accompanied by force on the ground as van after van of military and police officers screech into view and start piling out on to the ground, running into position around the rhinoceros and over by the bridge.

A flash of blue light causes me to shield my eyes and when I lower my arm, the only ones being surrounded are me and my animals.

The rhino and the elephant have vanished.

CHAPTER EIGHT

PRICELESS TIARA STOLEN!

Super animals cause Southbank destruction and make off with historic crown

A ROYAL FIASCO!

Opening night for the display of newly discovered tiara is an "embarrassment for Britain", as it is stolen in front of global guests.

Turn to page 2 for our full story, including an exclusive interview with Hollywood actor and eye-witness Maximillian Fringe:

"Luna Wolf let us down."

SUPER ANIMALS WILL BE OUR DOWNFALL

Why Luna Wolf must be stopped
A column by special correspondent Talia Tattle

Everyone thinks I did it.

OK, maybe not everyone – at least I have my family on my side. But I'm sure that every other person on the planet thinks that I masterminded the royal tiara heist and let my secret super animals loose as a distraction so I could get away with it.

The first few days after the party were *horrible*. I

was questioned by the police for ages while my dad sat next to me in the interview room furiously saying things like, "This is ridiculous! You saw her saving everyone!"

They even questioned Nan and I genuinely feel sorry for the officers who had to do that job. They emerged from the interview room looking extremely sheepish, while she swanned confidently out of the station.

As soon as Chief Inspector Reece heard we were being held, she came right on over and demanded we were released, pointing out that there was, in fact, no evidence to link me to the other three animals and reminding them of the many rescue missions I'd helped them with. But even she couldn't deny that I was the strongest suspect.

"I'm sure there's a simple explanation for all this," she'd said when we left to go home, but I saw her watching me with a wary expression as we pulled away in Dad's car.

Dad keeps saying everything will be fine, but I

found a business card for a defence lawyer in his coat pocket the other day.

The media is convinced that I've stolen the tiara. It has completely dominated the news and it's as though every journalist is out to get me. Hardly any of them have entertained the idea of other suspects and all they seem to be writing about is the police's failure to provide the evidence to lock me up.

It's as though the press has a personal vendetta against me and I have no idea why.

Social media has been flooded with eyewitness accounts describing my presence at the launch party, how I was at the front of the stage when the tiara was stolen, how I'm the only known person to be able to control super animals...

"The cheetah looked her right in the eye before it stole that tiara," Maximillian Fringe announced on a breakfast show the day after the robbery. "I'm certain it was looking to her for instruction and she was controlling it through her mind. She can say she's innocent all she likes, but I was there. I saw her. *I know she did it.*"

I'm a complete outcast at school and, worst of all, I get the feeling that even Ivy might think I'm guilty.

She's been acting strange around me since the incident, avoiding eye contact and being quieter than usual. When Kieron launched into a rant about how the press is giving me a hard time, I expected her to agree, considering she's always talked about how much she dislikes journalism. But instead, she blushed and made an excuse to leave.

I'm not sure I can blame her. I was at the event and I *do* have super animals. But I hoped she'd take my word for it. I don't want to have to persuade my friend that I'm innocent.

A week's holiday from school can't come soon enough. On the first Saturday evening of the half-term break, I climb on to my bed, sit back against my pillows, open the new book I borrowed from the school library and breathe a sigh of relief.

No school for a whole week.

That means no one staring at me in the corridors, whispering about me in classrooms, or shooting me dirty looks across the canteen.

"It's just us," I say out loud to the animals, who have come upstairs with me. "We have the entire week off," I continue cheerfully, as Silver hops up next to me on the bed, resting his head in my lap.

Chomp crawls up the stack of library books on the bedside table, while Stripes makes herself comfortable on my pillow. Blizzard is having fun jumping around my desk, speedily weaving around all my things, like it's an obstacle course set out for him, while Talon is stretching her wings outside, confined to Nan's garden.

"We can relax and no one will bother us," I say, turning to the first chapter of my book. "We're all alone and there's—"

"LUNA WOLF!"

I jump as my bedroom door swings open and Nan stands in the doorway, hands on her hips, bellowing my name as though I'm in trouble.

"Nan, what are you doing home? I thought you were at your a cappella class!"

"The choir master cancelled the lesson," she reveals, barrelling in. "He has lost his voice after watching his daughter take part in a football match. Apparently, he was shouting so much at the Ref, he got a yellow card."

"Spectators can be given yellow cards?"

"It would seem so." She crosses her arms. "More importantly, what are *you* doing home? I thought you were going to go to The Pumpkin Party!"

I look down at my book.

The Pumpkin Party is this big event taking place tonight in Covent Garden in London's West End. There are food and drink stalls, games, and a stage that's been erected in the piazza for musical entertainment, all to celebrate Halloween and the autumnal season. My favourite pop singer, Naomi Starr, is meant to be performing. Dad got us all tickets weeks ago and I've been looking forward to it for ages.

But after everything that's happened, there's no chance I'm going to a big public event. I told Kieron to give Ivy my ticket instead, so she's gone with him, Lucy and Dad. Kieron did try his best to persuade me to come, but I was adamant that it would be a disaster for everyone if I joined them, including him.

As disappointed as he was that I had to stay home, he promised that it wouldn't be for long – although he hasn't had much luck finding anyone online who used to work with Mum at Magnitude, he has heard back from Rex Robinson, who'd given him a small glimmer of hope of tracking someone down.

"Rex has been writing a piece on the Amazon rainforest," Kieron had informed me. "He's been doing research there and so been uncontactable. That's why it took him so long to reply. Anyway, he has no idea about the magical source or where it came from – apparently your mum never told him anything about it."

I'd sighed. "She was very secretive about her work."

"But," he'd said brightly, leaning in conspiratorially across the table, "he did remember something."

"What?"

"He said that Athena spoke about Callahan, obviously, but she also mentioned someone with a name beginning with 'J'. Jane or Jo or Josephine – he couldn't remember exactly, but he thinks it was something along those lines. Rex says she only mentioned her briefly as someone they could potentially trust."

"Does he remember her surname?" I'd asked hopefully.

Kieron had shaken his head. "Your mum mentioned her in passing once and never again after that. It was a long time ago."

"It's not much to go on," I'd said, deflated. "We don't even have a first name. Just that it begins with 'J'."

"Yeah, but it's *something*," he had emphasized. "We're one step closer to finding out the truth and proving your innocence, Luna."

Which was nice of him to say, but it doesn't feel like all that big a step. I'm still the only person in the frame for these attacks on the city.

"You were so excited about The Pumpkin Party," Nan says now, as I keep my eyes fixed on the open page in front of me. "Don't think I haven't noticed you staying inside all day. I thought you'd at least want to get out of the house this evening – it's the first day of your holiday! You're always in these days, hiding away from the world. It's not how it should be, Luna."

"Nan, remember what happened the last time I went to a big event in the middle of London," I say, raising my eyebrows at her. "It's better for everyone if I hide away until everything is better. My plan for the week is to have no plans."

"You're not honestly telling me that you intend to stay cooped up inside for the entirety of your half-term break," she says disapprovingly. "What about the rescue centre? Normally you'd jump at the chance to have free time on your hands to help Lucy out there."

"The rescue centre doesn't need me hanging around."

"Lucy always says how helpful you are!"

"How helpful I *was*," I correct. "Now, I come with a horde of reporters and photographers who stay all day, yelling things and trying to get a rise out of me or anyone I know. They would lurk by the entrance, putting people off from going in. Plus, I don't want the rescue centre to get any kind of negative publicity because I'm associated with it."

Nan takes in what I'm saying, her eyebrows knit together in concentration.

"Well … what about your friends?" she asks. "Don't you have any plans to see Kieron and Ivy this week?"

I shrug.

"You can't hide away in here forever," Nan says gently. "You deserve a holiday, like everyone else. Not to mention these poor animals deserve to get out and about. Tigers shouldn't be stuck inside on a pillow. They should be out in the wild, exploring!"

Stripes purrs loudly as I stroke her head.

"You mustn't care about what everyone out there thinks," Nan adds.

"It's hard not to care when it's all anyone can talk about."

Nan gives me a sympathetic look.

"I have faith that Chief Superintendent Reece and her team will find whoever's behind these attacks and clear your name," she declares resolutely. "In the meantime, we won't let them spoil our fun. How about we have our own Pumpkin Party right here at home? We can put on some pop music, whip up some delicious food and sit outside wrapped in blankets to drink hot chocolate with marshmallows."

"All right," I say enthusiastically, my evening starting to look up. "Maybe we can tell each other Halloween stories."

"Oh, I have many of those!" she tells me, rubbing her hands together. "My cousin twice-removed once told me about when he stayed in a haunted Scottish castle and, in the dead of night—"

She's interrupted by a crackling sound that comes from the corner of my desk.

"What's that?" she asks.

"It's the police radio, but it hasn't made a sound in weeks," I explain, as Nan wanders over to my desk and picks it up before Blizzard can knock it to the floor. "They don't want me to help with rescue missions any more because of everything that's happened."

The radio emits more crackles followed by a piercingly high-pitched sound that makes us all wince. Silver growls and the fur on Stripes's back stands on end.

"Why is it making that horrible noise?" Nan quickly passes it to me and then cups her hands over her ears. "Turn it off, Luna!"

"It's never done this before," I reason, as the sound finally stops. "Maybe it's because I haven't used it in so long, it's—"

A man's voice suddenly comes through the radio, loud and clear.

"Code Wolf," the voice instructs. "Incident at The Pumpkin Party in Covent Garden."

"The Pumpkin Party," Nan repeats, her eyes growing wide with fear.

I gasp, thinking of Dad, Lucy, Kieron and Ivy in the crowd. Silver whines, nudging me with his nose. My blue pendant begins to glow.

"High chance of danger. We need all hands on deck. Code Wolf. Code Wolf!" the voice says desperately.

"This is Luna Wolf," I reply into the radio without hesitation, swinging my legs out of bed. "We're on our way."

CHAPTER NINE

It takes so long to get to Covent Garden that I'm scared we'll be too late.

The roads surrounding the event have been closed off, so the traffic and public transport are completely jammed, and there are hundreds of people milling about the streets as excitable families make their way to the main stage and stalls of The Pumpkin Party. I'm surprised that I haven't been sent a police escort, which I've been lucky enough to get for my other rescue missions, but I assume they've needed the whole force to get to Covent Garden as soon as possible, rather than waste time picking me up. I'm just happy that they've called on me to help – maybe they do think I'm innocent.

As I weave through the crowd with Silver and Stripes striding alongside me, Chomp and Blizzard on my shoulders and Talon flying overhead, I get more and more nervous about the sight that will greet us when we arrive at the piazza.

"Tickets, please," a man wearing a hi-vis jacket says in a bored tone when I reach the barriers, not bothering to look up from scrolling through his phone.

"I don't have one," I tell him, craning my neck to see what's going on beyond him.

"Then, no entry," he states.

"But I need to get through!"

"Yeah, whatever." He snorts. "I've heard that all day long. If you don't have a ticket, you're not getting in."

I clear my throat pointedly.

Irritated, he glances up. The colour drains from his face.

"S-sorry," he squeals, jumping aside. "Please don't hurt me!"

I don't have time to explain that I'm here to help everyone, not hurt anyone. Barging past him, I stop to look around and work out where the danger is.

Everything seems strangely … normal.

No one is panicking. No one is screaming. No one is running away. The uplifting pop music is blaring through the speakers set up around Covent Garden as people, wrapped up warmly in coats and hats, meander through the stalls serving hot drinks and food. There are clusters of friends standing together, chatting and laughing. Families cheer each other on as they take part in the funfair-style games dotted around the place. The whole scene is fun and lively with no signs of any trouble whatsoever.

The only thing causing any kind of commotion is, well, me.

The guy in the hi-vis jacket has left his post, scarpering away into the crowd, and as others surrounding me start to notice I'm there, they begin to do the same. A ripple of whispers and gasps spreads through the piazza and I start to wonder whether I need to say something to assure everyone that I'm not here to cause trouble.

I grab the police radio from my pocket and speak into it.

"This is Luna Wolf, I'm at The Pumpkin Party in Covent Garden. Can someone tell me where the dangerous incident is?"

Noticing the scared expressions I'm causing, I wait anxiously for a reply. After a few moments of excruciating silence, a response comes.

"We haven't had any reports of a dangerous incident at The Pumpkin Party," a concerned woman's voice crackles through the radio.

"Yes, yes you have! You sent me here. I got a 'Code Wolf' message through my radio," I say, panicked.

"There has been no Code Wolf, I repeat, no Code Wolf," she insists. "Is this a warning call, Miss Wolf?"

"What? What do you mean?"

"Are you radioing in to report that you are about to cause a dangerous incident at The Pumpkin Party?"

"No! No, of course not! I was told to come here because people are in danger!"

"People are in danger at The Pumpkin Party? Are your animals out of control there?"

"No," I say clearly, trying to stay calm and controlled. "My animals are in control and... Look, I don't understand. You told me to come here! People are in danger!"

"All units to The Pumpkin Party at Covent Garden. I repeat, all units to The Pumpkin Party at Covent Garden! Luna Wolf is threatening to release super animals!"

I stare at the radio in disbelief, before holding it up to my mouth again.

"I'm not threatening anyone! I came here to help rescue people from a dangerous incident. But there must have been some kind of mistake because everything seems absolutely—"

Suddenly, a scream comes through the speakers, echoing around Covent Garden.

It's coming from the stage, where a band is half-way through their set. The drummer has leapt up from her stool and is shakily pointing at her drum kit. The rest of the band stop the performance and turn round to see what she's looking at.

A low, rumbling growl comes booming through the speakers as the head of a cheetah appears from behind the cymbals. With her back legs balanced on the bass drum and her front paws up on the snare, her fierce, wild eyes glimmer in the glare of the stage lights. She opens her jaws wide next to the microphone attached to the kit and lets out a threatening roar, her razor-sharp teeth on display.

The lead singer of the band spins round to face the audience and grabs her microphone.

"RUUUUUUN!" she screams into it, her voice echoing around the piazza.

Covent Garden erupts into chaos as the crowd disperses, everyone rushing in different directions, knocking over the barriers to clear the way, while others clamber over the front of their stall counters to escape. The cheetah meanwhile prowls the stage, her head dipped as she surveys the pandemonium below, as though she's calculating the best direction in which to pounce.

"You did this!" a man yells as he backs away from me. "Make it go away!"

"I can't!" I croak. "I didn't do this!"

As I desperately try to spot my dad in the confusion unfolding in front of me, a familiar face stands out from the crowd. Unlike everyone else, he's not moving. He's watching the cheetah and, although a little on edge, he doesn't look panicked or surprised.

"*Dean*," I whisper, clenching my fists when I see someone else I recognize creep over to stand next to him. "And Chad! I should have known!"

I'm about to march over to confront them when I'm distracted by the sound of thundering feet stampeding across cobblestones.

A shrill cry rises above the noise: "RHINO! Watch out!"

The rhinoceros seems to come from nowhere and charges into the side of the stage angrily and repeatedly, making the whole structure shake.

Silver nudges my leg urgently.

No, I communicate, shaking my head at him. *Everyone will think this is our fault again.*

He tilts his head at me. *We have to help.*

Silver, they could arrest us and take you all away from me, I tell him, wincing as the rhino charges the side of the stage again, causing a loud boom to echo off the walls.

No one will ever keep us apart, he insists.

People will hate me, I say.

His golden eyes flash at me. *Doing the right thing isn't always the easiest.*

His words suddenly make me think of Mum and what she had to do to rescue the animals from Magnitude. She must have felt so alone and scared of the consequences, but she knew she had to save them, so she found the courage to selflessly do so.

Silver knows what I'm thinking. When I look back at him, he whines.

I have to be brave like her, I tell him.

He barks confidently.

I check to make sure all the animals are ready and then shut my eyes, trying to drown out the sound of mass panic and disorder around me, bringing all my focus on my necklace. As the magic takes hold and I feel its warmth flowing through me, it's as though someone has turned the volume down on the rest of the world. The noise around me dims and I feel a sense of calm.

There's a blinding flash of blue light.

When I open my eyes, a wolf and tiger are at my side, a polar bear lets out a determined roar in front of me, a crocodile swishes his tail and chomps his jaws threateningly, and an eagle hovers in the air above, awaiting instruction.

"Here we go again," I say out loud, before giving them my instructions:

Protect the crowd! Distract the animals!

Talon swoops into action, soaring towards the cheetah and diving down right in front of her just like she did with the elephant on the Millennium Bridge. The cheetah hisses angrily and swipes at her with her claws, missing narrowly. She goes for Talon a second time as she dips closer and then quickly ascends, enjoying this fun game. It works: the cheetah is so busy concentrating on the eagle, she ignores the people scarpering around her.

Blizzard, Stripes and Chomp have made their way over to the rhino, who is still charging back and forth into the side of the stage. As my three animals form a semicircle around her, ready to stop her should she decide to channel her anger elsewhere, I feel a great sadness watching her slam into the structure. I think about what Blizzard communicated to me when he looked into the elephant's eyes. The rhino seems just as frustrated and confused: an animal trapped.

Blinking back tears, I glance at Silver.

He lets out a sombre whine.

I know, he says.

Silver and I are distracted by a small movement on the cobbled stones nearby and we both turn to observe a tiny object rolling towards us. As it lifts its head, its whiskers twitching, I realize it's not an object, but a mouse.

A searing blaze of light covers the piazza and when I squint through it, I see a dark shadow looming over me. I'm now standing in front of a giant elephant.

"Luna! Luna, watch out!" I hear Dad cry.

He appears next to me, grabbing my arm and gazing up at the elephant, his jaw falling open. Kieron, Ivy and Lucy follow close behind, flanking me as the elephant lifts his trunk and blows a trumpet sound that causes all of us to clap our hands round our ears.

"Where did he come from?" Kieron shouts.

"Someone here is controlling them," I say, desperately looking around for anyone who is still lingering. "There was a similar flash of light that comes from my necklace. Someone has the same magic!"

"I don't think anyone is controlling these animals," Lucy squeaks, clutching on to Dad. "Or if they are, they're not doing a very good job!"

Silver has launched himself in front of us and begins snarling and snapping at the elephant in warning. The elephant backs away, his stomping on the cobbles causing the whole of Covent Garden to feel like it's shaking.

I go to step forward, but my dad's hand tightens on my arm.

"What are you doing?" he asks, frowning.

"It's OK, Dad," I assure him. "I don't think that elephant wants to hurt anyone."

"But he might, whether he means to or not!"

"I have to try to get through to him. Dad, I *have to*."

Dad looks torn, but after a few moments, he relents. His grip loosens and I move to stand next to Silver. Appearing distressed, the elephant wobbles about on his feet, swinging his trunk through the air as he tries to make sense of his situation.

I hold up my hands and as he turns his head to look at me, I hold eye contact.

It's OK, I try to communicate. *I'm not going to hurt you.*

The elephant shakes his head. He doesn't believe me.

I promise. I want to help you, I say.

Following my lead, Silver stops growling and, instead, sits down.

His calmness has an immediate effect on the elephant, who stops stamping aimlessly at the ground and gradually becomes more at ease. As he settles, he looks deflated, weary and weak. With a flick of his ears, he bows his head.

It's going to be OK, I promise.

With Silver sticking to my side just in case, I edge towards the elephant and very slowly reach out my hand, my fingers outstretched…

A loud siren blares behind me. Before I can touch him, the elephant jumps back, his eyes wide with dismay, crashing backwards into stalls and causing a domino effect as they topple over, knocking over all the others around the piazza. More sirens and screeching car brakes pierce the evening air as dozens of police cars surround Covent Garden.

Before I can think what to do next, there's a blinding wash of blue light and the three wild animals that caused the chaos are gone.

An angry voice comes bellowing through a megaphone. "Luna Wolf! Stay where you are! Return your animals to their normal state."

Remaining a wolf, Silver stands protectively in front of me, baring his teeth at the officers taking their positions around the piazza.

"Are they going to arrest you?" Ivy asks quietly behind me. "We can't let them!"

"We won't," Dad says firmly.

"Maybe they'll believe Luna is innocent," Lucy says, but she doesn't sound convinced.

"It doesn't look good, Luna being at the scene of the crime again," Kieron admits.

"I was set up," I tell them angrily. "Someone wanted me to be here. They put me right in the centre of it all on purpose. Dean and Chad are involved with this. I saw them earlier."

"They're meant to be in prison!" Lucy exclaims.

"They're not any more," I inform her bitterly.

"No one can arrest you. They have no proof that any of this was to do with you," Dad states.

"They have me at the scene of the crime with my animals in tow," I point out. "There was also some radio miscommunication – the police officer I was speaking to thought I was threatening to attack The Pumpkin Party!"

"We can persuade them that you're nothing to do with this, Luna. We just need some time for everyone to" – Lucy glances worriedly at the approaching police officers and Chomp crawling towards them, his jaws wide open – "uh … calm down."

"I need to lie low somewhere," I say urgently, before running a hand through my hair. "Argh! I never should have left the house!"

"You're not a prisoner, Luna," Dad insists, looking upset. "It's going to be OK. We'll get everything straightened out. As Lucy says, all we need is time to—"

Dad doesn't get to finish his sentence, because we hear tyres screeching up the road behind us and spin round to see an old, muddy Land Rover pull up, braking suddenly next to us, the front passenger door swinging open.

"Luna, get in!" the driver instructs. "Richard, you'd better come, too."

I don't recognize the driver: a tall, gangly man in his late sixties with strikingly bushy eyebrows and thick, grey hair combed back from his face. He's wearing a bright orange-and-green floral bow tie and round tortoiseshell-framed glasses.

"It's OK, Luna," Kieron says excitedly behind me, before turning to address my dad. "Trust me! I promise it's OK. You two should go with the animals! Get out of here, quick!"

"But, what about the police?" Dad asks, bewildered.

"We'll handle them," Kieron answers confidently.

"You know where we'll be, Kieron," the driver says, as I slide into the passenger seat and Dad jumps in the back. Transforming back to their normal state, the animals pile into the car, too.

"I know," Kieron confirms. "We'll see you there."

He shuts the door behind me and the driver slams his foot on the accelerator. I watch Kieron, Lucy and Ivy grow smaller in the wing mirror as we speed away.

I turn to look at the driver.

"Hello, Luna, nice to meet you at last," he says, flashing a grin at me. "Rex Robinson, at your service."

CHAPTER TEN

Rex Robinson lives in a large, isolated house in the middle of the Hertfordshire countryside, miles from anyone or anything. It's so big that the furniture and valuable antiques in several of the rooms are covered in white sheets to protect them from dust. When Dad thanked him for the hundredth time for rescuing us from Covent Garden and bringing us to his home, Rex informed him that, frankly, he should be thanking us.

"It's nice to finally have some human company," he'd said.

Rex doesn't exactly live alone here – he has two

rescue dogs, some donkeys, chickens, llamas, and a couple of pigs. Aside from the dogs, his animals are supposed to all live outside in the purpose-built shelters and stables he's put up around his land, but he hasn't been able to stop them wandering into the house from time to time. The animals are the reason he still keeps this country manor and they were his purpose in coming home from his adventurous travels. He had people looking after them while he was away, but he missed them too much to stay out in the Amazon any longer.

"Sometimes I feel like they're the only ones who really get me," he'd told me and Dad whilst stroking the head of one of his rescue dogs, who was looking up at him adoringly. "It's as though they can read my mind."

Smiling down at Silver, I told Rex I knew how he felt.

We've only been here a couple of days and I already know exactly why Mum trusted Rex with her super animals once she'd rescued them from Magnitude.

He's devoted to his pets and he has the space to give them a wonderful life here. When Lucy and Kieron arrived at his house with Nan in tow the day after the Pumpkin Party debacle, Lucy and Rex got chatting about her rescue centre and Rex declared he'd love to do an article on the centre to raise funds for it. He's as passionate about animals as Mum was.

The animals love him and haven't forgotten how well he looked after them – as soon as we'd parked at his house and climbed out of the car, Silver jumped up and down at Rex, covering him in slobbery licks and making him laugh, while Stripes purred loudly, rubbing her back against his leg, vying for his attention. Talon launched into her signature celebratory somersaults above his head and Blizzard hopped up on to Stripes to use her as a launching pad to jump into Rex's cradled arms. Chomp was desperate to get to him and when I passed him over, Rex lifted Blizzard up on to his shoulder so he could hold the gecko in his cupped hands and start cooing to him.

We're staying with Rex for the rest of half term.

He insisted on it and neither Dad nor I were tempted to say no. It's like I've escaped the world here and I can finally breathe. Everything is quiet and peaceful, and I don't feel like I need to hide – I can walk through the fields with the animals and I don't need to worry about bumping into anyone and scaring them away. I can be myself again.

The day after The Pumpkin Party, Chief Superintendent Reece paid us a visit. We knew she was coming because she'd been to see Nan, Lucy and Kieron the night before, asking about my whereabouts and explaining that she wasn't going to arrest me – she just wanted to talk. Not wanting them to lie on our behalf, Dad decided to get in touch with her directly to let her know where we were. She was true to her word and didn't put me in handcuffs – although, even if she'd wanted to, it would have been very difficult because Silver stood in between us the entire time she was here. Any time she glanced down at him, he gave a small but audible warning growl.

On Dad's encouragement, I explained to her exactly what had happened: how I'd heard the Code Wolf through the radio, arrived to find everything was fine, and then seen the animals transform in front of my eyes before directing my super animals to protect the crowds of people. Chief Superintendent Reece listened patiently to my account of events.

"It is interesting that you happened to be there," she couldn't help but comment, eyeing me up suspiciously.

"Interesting?" Rex had repeated, raising his eyebrows at her. "Surely you mean, it's *worrying*."

"Worrying that Luna was at the scene of the crime?" she'd said, confused.

"Worrying that someone was able to hack into the police system and contact Luna through your equipment to feign a fake 'Code Wolf' message without your knowledge in a sophisticated attempt to frame her," he'd corrected.

She'd looked embarrassed. Dad had given Rex a grateful smile.

Even with Rex's support, I'm not sure if the Chief Superintendent is convinced of my innocence. I suppose it's her job to keep an open mind and follow the facts she has, but I'd like to think that my helping out with all those rescue missions has shown her that I'm not the sort of person to let a pet rhinoceros loose in London for a bit of fun. As Dad said to her yesterday, *why* would I do something like that?

Still, I'm glad we were with Rex when she came to question me. He had my back during her interview and was very reassuring after she'd left. At least while I'm here in the countryside, I can't be blamed for anything that happens in the city.

Unlike in London, there might be a chance I can relax here. Dad has taken some time off work, Lucy has asked one of her employees to take charge of the rescue centre for the week, and Nan has informed all the various people who run the many classes she takes that she's having a break this week. She did ask Rex if he would mind her practicing her aerial yoga here, though, and he said it was no problem as long as she didn't attach any of her silk fabrics to the chandeliers in the old ballroom.

Rex has fished out all the animals' old things that he's been storing away in the attic and placed them around the sitting room, so that on Monday evening when we head in there after dinner, the animals can make themselves comfortable. There's a plush cushion for Stripes on one of the armchairs, a log that Chomp likes to explore, and a beautiful hand-crafted bird box for Talon to rest in when she gets back from her evening flying. Blizzard has been scurrying around the room busily, but once Rex has finished lighting the fire, he comes scampering over and positions himself snugly on Rex's shoulder.

"It really is very kind of you to let us stay here," Lucy says, clasping a mug of mint tea.

"I wouldn't mind all of you moving in permanently if it means more meals like that one," Rex says, smiling at Nan, who chuckles and waves off the compliment. "Thank you so much for cooking, Clementine. You must give me the recipe for your Caribbean fish pie."

"It's my pleasure, the least I can do with you hosting us for the week," she says, sitting down at his insistence in one of the red velvet wingback chairs by the fireplace. "Your kitchen is magnificent. I've never had so many stoves to choose from!"

"They're barely used, I'm afraid," Rex admits. "When I'm travelling, there's no one here to make use of the kitchen, and if I am at home, then I'm only cooking for me, so I never really bother going to too much effort, especially if I'm in the middle of writing an article. Once I start writing, it's hard for me to concentrate on anything else."

"I'm the same," Kieron says, admiring the grand piano in the corner of the room.

"If Kieron is at his laptop writing, then I know not to speak to him," Lucy says, chuckling. "I can try asking him a question, but even if he answers, I know he's not really concentrating on anything I'm saying. I call it his 'writing haze'. If he's in it, I try not to disturb him until he's out."

Watching Talon soaring over the paddock through the window on the far side of the room, I feel a pang in my chest. At first, I can't understand why I feel this way, and then I slowly realize it's because I never really see Talon look this exultant in London. She gets to flit around a bit, sure, but out there, above the open countryside, she's really flying.

Silver nudges my hand with his wet nose, making sure I know he's there.

Talon looks free, I tell him.

He sits down and leans against my leg. With him at my side, the pang ebbs away.

Returning my attention to the room, I notice Rex watching me, his eyes gleaming with tears and his forehead lined with sadness.

"Sorry," Rex croaks, collecting himself. "I don't mean to get upset. It's just … well, it's like Athena is here in this room again. Your bond with that dog – I've seen it before with your mum. You really are so like her."

Dad smiles at the observation and, standing beside Nan's chair, reaches out to place a hand on her arm. Looking down at the ground, she pats his hand comfortingly.

A thought springs into my mind.

"Rex, what did my mum call Silver?" I ask excitedly. "Ever since I found out that Silver once belonged to her, I've wanted to know because he got the name Silver once he arrived at the rescue centre. Callahan told me that at Magnitude he was called Animal Number Five, but I don't believe Mum wouldn't have given him a name."

"You're right," Rex says, grinning. "When Athena brought him here, she told me his name was Shep."

"Wow." I stroke his head. "That's a lovely name. Do you think we should be calling him that instead? I've grown so used to 'Silver', but I'd hate to think that wasn't the name he really wants."

"Why don't you ask him?" Nan suggests.

"What do you think, mister?" I say, stroking his head. "Are you happy with Silver or—?"

He doesn't let me finish the sentence, jumping up at me and barking happily.

"Silver it is!" Rex laughs. "Athena would have approved of that name, I'm sure. You know, it doesn't seem like it's been seven years since she was here. Time certainly flies!"

"What was it like, rescuing the animals from Magnitude?" Kieron asks eagerly.

"I was hardly involved," Rex replies, leaning against the mantelpiece. "It was all Athena. She was the heroic one. I simply helped to organize the helicopter to aid in her escape and then offered the animals a home once she'd got them out of there. Your mum was the one who took the risk. She really was one of the bravest people I'd ever met, Luna. I'm not sure many people would have the courage to go up against the people behind Magnitude. They were very powerful."

"You mean Callahan?" Lucy asks.

Rex shakes his head. "Dr Gerry Callahan was one of the scientists behind Magnitude, but he wasn't the one financing it and pulling the strings."

"I bet he's involved again this time round," I seethe. "I saw Dean and Chad in Covent Garden – they used to work for him. If they're out of prison, Callahan might be, too."

"I wouldn't be surprised," Rex says, tickling the top of Blizzard's head with his forefinger.

Dad looks confused. "Why? Do you think he made a good enough excuse for his behaviour to get a shorter sentence? He is clever enough to be a good liar."

"Maybe he had a brilliant lawyer," Lucy suggests.

"No, no, it's much more than that," Rex says, his brow furrowed. "Callahan is in the pocket of someone who needs his expertise. Someone who is likely intent on rebooting Magnitude."

"We figured it might be the same people behind these recent attacks who were involved in Magnitude long ago," Kieron says. "That's why I asked you whether you remembered any of Athena's colleagues."

"It was smart thinking," Rex acknowledges. "I'm sorry I couldn't be more help. If only I had written down the name! I've been through all the notes I took down at the time but there's nothing in there. I remember Athena talking about this person as if she felt a little sorry for them – I think a lot of people didn't think they were good enough. But Athena could see potential. It was someone who worked alongside her; a friend."

Dad frowns. "It can't have been Callahan."

"No, this was someone else," Rex recalls, shutting his eyes as though that might help him remember the details. "Come on, Rex, *think*! A young Magnitude scientist who really looked up to her. I remember being shocked when she said there was only one person at Magnitude who she might be able to trust. Although, of course, in the end she decided it best not to get them involved just in case things went awry … *argh*. Why can't I remember something so important?"

"How were you to know their name was important?" Lucy says gently. "It's been seven years; you can't be expected to remember every detail."

"Sometimes, if I need to remember something I know I've forgotten, I lie on the grass, inhale deeply through my nose, clear my mind and eat a blueberry," Nan says wisely.

Kieron suppresses a snigger. She glares at him and he shuts up immediately.

"I'm telling you it works," she insists, turning her focus back to Rex. "My mother once forgot the whereabouts of our family's buried treasure. She ate a blueberry and the location came right back to her. You can try it tomorrow."

"I would, but I don't have any blueberries," Rex says regretfully.

"Not to worry, I'll track some down for you. A deep breath and a blueberry," she repeats sternly. "It's all you need to jolt your memory."

"Hang on a minute, Nan," I say, intrigued. "What's this about our family's buried treasure?"

She chuckles, taking a sip of her drink. "That's a story for another time."

The next day, we're enjoying a quiet, lazy afternoon in the sitting room when Rex suddenly comes bursting in through the door breathing heavily, his cheeks flushed.

"Joanna!" he bellows at me.

We all stare at him in silence.

"Uh … no, my name is Luna," I say awkwardly.

"No, no, no," he says, marching over to me with a beaming smile. "Joanna is the name of your mum's colleague! The one she mentioned that time! *Joanna*."

I jump to my feet. "Are you sure?"

"Yes!" He nods vigorously. "I was lying on the grass, I ate a blueberry and her name popped into my head!"

"You're joking," Kieron says in disbelief.

"I told you!" Nan says smugly.

"I know it's not much to go on, it's only her first

name," Rex says, stroking his chin. "But it's better than nothing, right?"

"Of course," I assure him. "We can go through everything we've discovered so far on Magnitude and see if someone called 'Joanna' crops up anywhere. Hopefully it will get us one step closer to finding out the truth! Thank you, Rex."

"To be honest, Luna, I'm not sure the truth would help when it comes to clearing your name," Kieron says, his forehead creased in concentration as he spreads the papers out across the grand piano.

Rex told Kieron that it's important to read every newspaper if he wants to be a serious journalist – by reading about the same story in different publications, he can understand how bias works and ultimately establish the truth for himself. He needs to see the same issue from different angles. Kieron is taking his guidance very seriously and has spent all day studying the headlines and opinion columns.

"It seems like specific papers really have it in for you," he continues, glancing up from the papers.

"I noticed it yesterday and there's a similar pattern today. Come take a look."

We all gather round him, peering over his shoulder as he gestures to specific newspapers while he makes his point. "These four are accusing you in their top headlines, whereas these three newspapers are more focused on international news as their lead stories – the super animals are front page, but they're lower down and all it says is that there have been no updates from the police force."

"Very interesting, Kieron!" Rex exclaims, patting his shoulder proudly.

"That's weird," I say.

Kieron frowns. "I think someone might be running a smear campaign against you, Luna. All along I've felt that it was weird how negative the media has been. These newspapers are intentionally pointing the finger at you and trying to destroy your reputation. If you read their articles, it's like there are no other suspects at all! Whereas some of the smaller papers are just reporting the facts."

"You're saying that the editors of these papers are out to get Luna." Nan puts her hands on her hips. "But *why*?"

"Because having a named suspect is much more interesting than reporting that the police still don't have any leads," Dad guesses.

"Hang on a second," Rex says, examining the papers that have it in for me. "There's a link between these four. They're all owned by the same person!"

Kieron gasps. "Sarah Slade."

"The millionaire?" Lucy checks.

"Try *billionaire*," Rex informs her. "She controls a media empire, including all those papers and, now that I think about it, a lot of platforms that have been equally accusatory about Luna and the super animals." He pauses, looking at me thoughtfully. "Kieron may be on to something. I think Sarah Slade is running a direct smear campaign about you, Luna."

"Why would she do that?" Dad asks angrily,

clenching his fists. "What reason would she have to go after Luna?"

The doorbell goes and Nan offers to go answer it.

"It doesn't make sense," Kieron says, frowning as he types Sarah Slade's name into his phone and starts clicking on the articles about her.

"You don't know her, do you, Luna?" Rex asks curiously.

I shake my head. "No! We've never met."

"She doesn't have any connection to our family," Dad asserts.

Poring over an interview with Sarah Slade, Kieron suddenly jolts his head up, looking as though he's been slapped across the face.

"What is it?" I ask him urgently. "What's wrong?"

"In this article, the media tycoon Sarah Slade talks about her daughter," he croaks, the colour draining from his face.

Lucy shares a confused look with Dad.

"And?" she prompts.

"Sarah Slade's daughter is called Ivy," he says, turning his phone and holding up the screen so that we can see a photo of Sarah and her daughter. "Ivy Campbell-Slade."

I feel like all the breath has been knocked out of my body.

"Luna, Kieron, I have a surprise for you!" Nan trills, stepping back into the room and gesturing to the person following her in. "Look who's arrived!"

CHAPTER ELEVEN

"I can explain everything," Ivy begins, placing her bag down on the floor after seeing the photo of her and her mum up on Kieron's phone.

"Your mum is Sarah Slade, the owner of all these newspapers and websites that have been dragging Luna's name through the mud," Kieron says, gesturing to the headlines on the papers spread across the piano.

Ivy swallows audibly. "Yes."

"Why wouldn't you tell us that?" I ask, my face growing hot. "Was our friendship fake? Did she ask you to get close to me to find out stories that would sell?"

"No!" she exclaims, looking hurt at the accusation. "We *are* friends."

"But you lied to us and you let your mum write these horrible things about your friend," Kieron says, rubbing his forehead as though trying to make sense of it all. "The press has been making Luna's life a misery! Why wouldn't you say something?"

"I didn't know how to tell you," Ivy begins, her eyes gleaming. "I was scared that you'd think badly of me when you found out and—"

"All those things you said about disliking irresponsible journalism, were they a ruse so I wouldn't find out who you really are?" I ask, the anger bubbling up inside me.

"No, I meant every word I said," she insists. "I've grown up knowing exactly how people like my mum can twist stories to suit her opinions. That's why I would never trust any of her publications." She looks pleadingly at me. "Luna, you have to believe that I would never want to hurt you, you're my friend. I don't get on with my mum, I barely see

203

her…" She hesitates. "Or rather, she never sees me. She left me and Dad years ago after trying to destroy his reputation in the press and our relationship was never the same again. I don't agree with her way of doing things."

"But you're still in contact with her?" I ask sharply.

"A little," she admits. "She's my mum."

"Did you mention you're friends with me? Did you ask her to stop printing all those lies and mean things about me? Did you tell her to stop trying to turn absolutely everyone in the world against me?"

Dad attempts to place a calm hand on my shoulder, but I shake him off.

"Luna," he says softly, "maybe we should all take a deep breath and talk about—"

"I couldn't tell her that I was friends with you, Luna, because then she might try to use me to get to you," Ivy explains with a hint of bitterness. "You don't know what she's like. She'll do anything for a story – she'll align herself with the worst kind of people just to make sure that her papers sell. I'm not like her."

"Of course you're not," Nan says kindly, before appealing to me. "Luna, perhaps you can understand why Ivy didn't tell you any of this before."

"I don't understand," I say, the tears spilling over and running down my cheeks. "I don't understand at all."

I storm out of the room with Silver hot on my heels and run down the hall and out through the door into the garden. Slowing down, I keep walking until I'm at the end of the field where the donkeys are grazing and I slump on to the grass, even though it's cold and wet from earlier rain. Silver sits next to me, and I put my arms around him. I hold him tight, burying my face in his fur.

Maybe my exit was a little overdramatic, but I had to get out of that stifling room. My head was whirring from this new information. All this time, Ivy, who has become one of my best friends, has seen how those headlines have hurt me, known that I've been shutting myself away from everyone, too scared of their opinions, which have been shaped by the media, and never ONCE thought to mention to me that her MUM was the person behind all of it?! How could she have kept this secret from me?

Silver sighs heavily.

"I know," I say, lifting my head and wiping my cheeks. "Everything is rubbish."

I hear footsteps behind me and turn to see Dad approaching. Thankfully, he's on his own. I don't say anything as he steps across the grass and then plonks himself down next to me. He quickly makes a face.

"The grass is wet," he observes, then shrugs. "Oh well. At least we'll *both* look like we've wet ourselves."

A small chuckle bubbles up my throat.

"Ah, I made you laugh. That's a good start," he notes positively.

I give him a look. "Did you come out here to lecture me on storming out the room?"

He shakes his head. "No, I can understand why you did that. Everyone can. Sometimes it's important to take yourself out of a situation so you can properly process it. That was a bit of a bombshell back there and it makes sense that you'd need a bit of time and space."

Dad pauses to take a deep breath, readying himself to continue.

"You've gone through a lot the last few months, Luna," he says, gazing out across the tranquil countryside. "You've had to come to terms with this magical side of you and your abilities to connect to the super animals, which can be a lot for someone your age. For someone any age, for that matter. But on top of that, there's all the other stuff too."

"What stuff?"

"Leaving your old school to go to a new one. Moving from the middle of nowhere to a big city. Living with Nan while we look for a new house. Your dad dating someone new. Accepting that someone and her son." He smiles at me. "That's a *lot* of change to handle."

I shrug. "Some of it is good change."

"I know, but that doesn't take away from how daunting it is. And the thing is, Luna, you've been so mature about it all that sometimes I forget how much you're dealing with. I want you to know that if you ever want to talk about anything, if you're feeling overwhelmed or if you're uncomfortable with something, you can come and talk to me about it." He holds up his hands, the palms of which have bits of wet grass and mud stuck to them. "There will be no judgement or anger. We can talk through it together and work it out. I don't want you to ever feel as though you have to deal with something alone. OK?"

I nod slowly. "OK. Thanks."

"Thank *you*. And I don't just mean the family stuff, I mean the Animal Wizard things, too. We can talk about anything."

I smile to myself. "Kieron told you that's the title he gave me?"

"I like it. Better than the Super Animal Adventurers or whatever it was the press came up with when you went viral the first time."

I bury my head in my hands. "Argh. If only that hadn't happened. Then I could have kept the animals a secret and no one would have noticed me. No one would think I'd stolen a priceless Tudor tiara or think I'm out to destroy Covent Garden."

Pausing, I feel tears pricking at my eyes again and add quietly, "When I think about everything Mum did, everything she sacrificed, to keep the animals safe and secret, I feel like I've let her down."

Dad's jaw clenches and he takes a moment before he speaks.

"Do you really think you could have kept the animals secret forever?" he says eventually. "I'm surprised we managed it as long as we did. News of this magic was always going to come out sooner or later; it's what you did next that matters. And *look what you did.*"

I sniff. "What? Ended up as the country's Most Wanted?"

He laughs, shaking his head. "You used the magic to save people. You didn't use it to gain power or money or fame or popularity. When people needed help, you were there. I can tell you with great confidence that you haven't let your mum down. You've honoured everything she did and more. I know she's proud of you, Luna. I only wish she were here to tell you yourself."

As he concludes, he reaches over to swipe away the tear rolling down my cheek.

"Thanks, Dad," I say, my voice wobbling.

He smiles and we sit in silence for a moment, watching the donkeys mill about in front of us. Silver lies down next to me and puts his head between his paws, closing his eyes as I place my hand on his head.

"You know," Dad says suddenly, interrupting the peace, "as much as you are like your mum, none of us are our parents. We are all our own person."

I furrow my brow. "Yeah, I know."

"You're not your mum. Ivy's not hers either," he says pointedly.

"Oh. Right." I exhale, scratching the soft bit behind Silver's ears.

"Do I have your permission to offer my opinion on the matter?"

"Go ahead. My brain is a muddle, so any advice might help."

"Ivy should have told you from the start. Even though she was worried about what you might think or embarrassed about her connection, she should have trusted you. Instead, by keeping it from you, she betrayed your trust in her."

"Very well put," I remark.

"Thank you," he grins. "However, everyone makes mistakes, right? When we care about someone and how they'll react, we naturally want to protect them. Sometimes that can lead to making the wrong decision, especially if we're worried that the way they see us will change and affect the friendship. Doesn't that make sense?"

"I suppose."

"Personally, I think Ivy is brave. It's hard to have completely different principles to your family, it must cause her a lot of upset. We can't choose our parents.

Ivy's mum is a very powerful person – think how easy it would be to agree with her and accept all the wins that come your way if you do. Instead, Ivy chooses to be true to herself and go against what her mum stands for. I have to admire her for that."

Silver lifts his head and whines.

"Us too," I translate for Dad.

"So, maybe you might consider forgiving her for not telling you about her mum?" Dad asks hopefully.

"I think I will," I decide.

He smiles in relief. "Good, because I invited her to stay for the week and it would have been very awkward if you two weren't speaking."

I throw my head back and laugh.

"What would you have done if I'd said 'no'?" I ask.

"This may come as a surprise, but I happen to know a little about my daughter," he answers, putting his arm round my shoulders and pulling me into him. "You've never been good at holding a grudge. Now, can I suggest we go back inside?

My bum is completely soaked from sitting on this grass."

I agree that it would be best and he stands up first before reaching down to grab my hand and haul me up on my feet. We start strolling back to the house with Silver plodding along next to me.

"I miss this," Dad blurts out as we walk.

"This is the first time we've come here," I say, frowning in confusion.

"No, I mean us hanging out together, the two of us," he explains. "Our house is very crowded in London and with work and my relationship with Lucy, we haven't spent much time just us together, have we? That's my fault."

"It's not your fault, Dad. I've been busy with school and rescue missions and … avoiding arrest," I joke, making him chortle. "But I miss it too."

"How about when we get home, we schedule in some evenings to do something fun together? Go bowling or try out a new restaurant or go to the cinema. That sound like a good plan?"

"Yeah," I say, grinning up at him. "It sounds like a great one."

Ivy and I spend a long time apologizing to each other.

She keeps saying how sorry she is for keeping such a big secret from me. I say sorry for saying all those things in anger to her when she arrived and then storming out in front of everyone. Then she jumps back in to say sorry for all the horrible headlines her mum's media empire has unleashed upon the world and how embarrassed she is. I reply that I'm sorry for blaming her for something that is completely out of her control and for her feeling like she couldn't talk to us about it.

Then she begins to apologize for something else, but she doesn't get the chance because Kieron buts in. "Can you both PLEASE just accept you're both sorry and hug it out so I don't have to listen to any more of this?"

We accept his point and wrap things up, giving each other a big hug.

"I won't keep a secret from you again, I promise," Ivy says, as she pulls away from me and goes to perch on the twin bed next to mine.

We've left Dad, Rex and Nan downstairs while we talk through everything up here in the room I'm staying in. There are a lot of spare rooms in Rex's big house, but I picked this one because there's a framed picture on the wall of a wolf that Rex took on one of his visits to Alaska, so it seemed appropriate for Silver and me to sleep in here.

"I can't believe you're Sarah Slade's daughter," Kieron remarks. "If I wasn't so angry at her right now, I'd be begging you to get me an internship somewhere."

"Trust me, you're too good to work at any of her publications," Ivy assures him.

"Now I know why you were so knowledgeable

when it came to our debates about the press. It's a little embarrassing that I didn't work out who you were sooner," he says.

She smiles. "A little. Call yourself an investigative journalist."

"Hey, you dropped the 'Slade' from your surname on purpose," he points out.

"Wouldn't you?" she says with a shrug. "After what happened at my last school, I wanted to start with a new slate when I arrived at our one last year. But then the bin thing happened, so I hardly got off to a good start."

"What happened at your old school?" I ask.

She sighs, raising her eyes to the ceiling. "When my parents split up, it was pretty big news and then an article was published talking about how my dad was this social-climbing gold digger who had schemed to marry and then divorce my mum so he could have her fortune. The piece included loads of personal details about my dad and his family that no one else knew about – not very nice stuff. The journalist who wrote the piece said he got all his information from a 'secret source close to the family'. Hardly a secret who that source was: my mum owned the paper the article ran in."

"That's horrible," I say, feeling a wave of sympathy for her.

"It wasn't great. Anyway, everyone at my last school knew about it and there were some bullies who would tease me about my dad a lot. I kept asking him if I could change schools and he finally listened to me."

"After that experience, no wonder you didn't want people to know who your parents were." Kieron nods. "I would have felt exactly the same."

"I should have trusted you sooner," she says, before giving me an apologetic look. "When you first arrived at school and that video had gone viral, I felt that I knew a little about what you were going through: feeling like everyone knows your business and is talking about you. That's why I wanted to make friends. I never set out to trick you."

"I know," I assure her. "You don't have to explain any more, I completely understand why you kept it from us. And if it means anything, I promise that now we know, it doesn't change a thing about the way we see you."

She smiles gratefully at me.

Kieron checks his watch and then jumps to his feet.

"Right, now that that's all sorted, I'm going to get to work," he announces, turning to explain himself to Ivy. "We've had a major breakthrough with Magnitude."

She brightens. "You have? What is it?"

"Rex remembers the name of one of Athena's colleagues!"

"Brilliant! What is it?" she asks eagerly.

He takes a deep breath before announcing it. "Joanna."

She waits, expecting more, so when it doesn't come, she prompts him, "Joanna *what*?"

"We don't know her surname," he confirms.

Her shoulders slump in disappointment. "All you have to go on is 'Joanna'?"

"OK, so maybe calling it a major breakthrough is a slight exaggeration," he concedes, holding up his finger, "but it is a breakthrough all the same. I'm going to go get my laptop and do some digging into any scientist out there who specializes in veterinary medicine development, has a mysterious past and is named Joanna. Wish me luck!"

"Good luck," Ivy calls out after him, adding quietly so he can't hear, "I have a feeling you're going to need it."

During the night, I'm woken up by Kieron prodding my shoulder with his finger.

"Luna. *Luna!* Wake up."

I groan, my eyelids heavy with sleep as I peer up at him. I can see the dim glow of his screen as he balances his laptop on top of my duvet.

"What time is it?" I croak, confused.

"It's one o'clock in the morning."

"Then why am I awake?" I moan, pulling the duvet over my head.

"Because I found her," he answers, yanking it back from me.

"Found who?" I huff, rubbing my eyes.

"Joanna," he says, and I can hear the joy in his voice as he tells me. "Dr Joanna Gild, who worked at Magnitude with your mum."

I prop myself up on my elbows.

"Are you… Are you serious?"

"Yes, and I contacted her on the off chance," he whispers, sounding like he hardly dares to believe what he's saying. "She wrote back. She wants to meet."

CHAPTER TWELVE

"'There are some out there, like Dr W, whose work will never be fully lauded as it should and whose potential we will never have the honour of seeing realized. It was a privilege to work with her on such a super project. Now, moving on to my aforementioned point about stem cell therapy, it must be acknowledged that' … oh—" Kieron pauses in the middle of reading aloud the article and looks up at his captive audience. "The rest isn't relevant. So, there you go!"

Gathered in Rex's kitchen the next morning, we all watch him, captivated. Nan was cooking breakfast but stopped when Kieron announced that he'd found the "Joanna" that my mum had mentioned to Rex several years ago. Dad and Lucy are clutching their mugs of coffee, looking in awe of him, while Ivy claps her hands in excitement. Rex isn't here yet; Nan told us that he was up bright and early and has already been outside for a while tending to all his animals. I can't wait for him to hear Kieron's news.

"You're telling me that that *tiny* passage – those couple of sentences – in a random article on veterinary stem cell therapy is how you found her?" Dad asks, walking over to clap Kieron on the back. "You really are *brilliant*, Kieron."

Kieron flushes, adjusting his glasses.

"Not really; it's strange I didn't find this sooner," he says modestly. "I simply changed what I was searching for. Rather than focusing on Magnitude, I tried looking for mentions of Athena, and then I realized that she'd be referred to as Dr Wolf professionally. When I combined that with using the search terms relevant to Magnitude – 'super', 'animals', 'magic' and so on, this paragraph popped up. I'm sure I would have searched those terms before but somehow I must have missed this."

"It's amazing you found this at all," Lucy says, beaming proudly at him. "Well done, Kieron! You are a superstar."

"I still should have come across it when I first started researching Magnitude and Athena's work," he says, his eyebrows furrowed. "I'm pleased I found it now, but also annoyed I didn't discover it before. There are some big clues – I think Joanna described the project as 'super' on purpose."

"You think she hoped someone would track her down?" I ask, surprised.

"Maybe. It seems an odd use of the word in such a formal article." He shrugs. "The question is whether she wanted that someone to expose Magnitude or reignite it."

"Let's hope it's the former," Nan remarks.

"So, where does she want to meet?" Dad says, taking a sip of his coffee.

"Who wants to meet?" asks Rex, entering the

kitchen in his coat, his cheeks red and ruddy from the fresh air. His two dogs bound in alongside him and start trying to play with Silver. "It's a chilly day out there! All the animals have been fed, which is no easy task when there's a certain ferret trying to steal the food as soon as I put it out. The llamas are not his biggest fans – he had to dodge a lot of spit."

Blizzard emerges from Rex's coat and bounds along the table towards me, causing a racket as he jumps on the plates and cutlery, and knocking over the vase of flowers Nan had put out this morning. Dad catches it just in time before it smashes.

"Whoops!" I say, giving Dad a grateful smile. "He's not the most elegant of ferrets."

"True, but he does love it out in the open," Rex says, moving to the sink to wash his hands. "He was scurrying all over the place, having the time of his life. We saw Talon, too. She's playing with the other birds in the trees."

"Talon is *playing*?" I look at him aghast. "That doesn't sound like her."

"She's too snooty to play," Dad remarks.

"Maybe the fresh country air brings out her playful side," Rex says. "She's gliding on the breeze with a bunch of fellow sparrows, helping them look for seeds and insects. Which reminds me, I must top up the bird feeders today."

"Has anyone seen Chomp?" I say, trying to ignore the mixed emotions I'm feeling about how noticeably happier Blizzard and Talon seem to be in the countryside.

"Oh!" Rex dips his hand into his pocket and holds out Chomp, who is fast asleep. "He's exhausted from this morning, so I tucked him away for a little kip."

"What was this morning?" I ask curiously.

"I found him in the fruit bowl when I came downstairs early and he looked like he was having fun climbing the different items—"

"Yes, he likes to do that," Nan interrupts, rolling her eyes. "He likes to give guests a fright when they open cupboard doors and find him perching on mugs."

"I thought he might enjoy the outdoors for a bit,"

Rex tells us, "so I took him with me when I went to sort the donkeys and I let him have a play down by the stream that runs alongside their field. There's lots of rocks there. He had a marvellous time exploring! I'll go pop him on his log in the sitting room so he can have a snooze there."

Rex turns to leave and then pauses, swivelling back around. "Hold on, I've got distracted. When I came in you were saying something about someone wanting to meet."

"Kieron found Joanna," Lucy says, smiling into her mug.

Rex's eyes widen with hope as he turns to Kieron for an explanation.

"Dr Joanna Gild," Kieron tells him, moving round the table to show Rex the article still up on his phone. "She worked at Magnitude with Athena. I messaged her last night to check and she's confirmed it. I've persuaded her to meet us."

"Excellent work, Kieron, first rate journalism!" Rex cries.

While Kieron was pleased with our praise, it's obvious from his overjoyed expression that his mentor's comments mean a lot to him.

"Does she want to meet in London?" Nan asks, returning her attention to her dish and sprinkling in some pepper. "She'd be welcome to come to our house."

"I don't think that's a good idea," Kieron says. "We want to meet somewhere neutral – remember, we have no idea what Joanna knows. We know Athena trusted her but she's still a former employee of Magnitude; maybe she didn't end up sharing the same values as your mum, Luna. We have to be cautious. Plus, reporters might still be hanging around your house, Clementine, hoping Luna will return soon."

"They had better not be stamping about my lawn when I'm not there to supervise," Nan grumbles.

"What about the rescue centre?" Lucy suggests, folding her arms and leaning back against the counter. "We could ask her to meet us there."

"Maybe, but it still seems risky for the same

reasons," Kieron says apologetically. "It's only down the road from Clementine's and the press know the link to Luna."

"How about a café?" Dad says.

Kieron sighs. "Too public. Everyone knows who Luna is now. The meeting will be up on social media in seconds."

"I could go in disguise," I offer.

"You'd still have to make sure your conversation was very private."

The room falls into silence as we all try to think of somewhere suitable.

"What about my house?" Ivy pipes up.

Kieron turns to her, intrigued. "Your house?"

"It would be private and neutral, and the press wouldn't think to go there looking for Luna," she points out.

"That's very kind, Ivy, but what about your dad?" Lucy says. "We wouldn't want to intrude, and I'd hate for him to feel he's become involved in any of this."

Ivy snorts. "You don't need to worry about that. He's at the house in Cyprus. When I said I was getting on the train to come here, he booked the first flight he could get on."

"When will he be back?" Lucy asks at the same time that Kieron says, "You have a house in Cyprus?"

Ivy smiles. "Yes, we have a house there, and I have no idea when he'll be back. He'll just let me know, I guess." She notices everyone's shocked expressions and gives a wave of her hand, as though brushing our concern away. "He always sends someone to check on me, so I'm not alone in the house. He's just not exactly a 'hands-on' parent. He's got a very exciting social life that involves a lot of international travel to glitzy events. It's OK, I'm used to it. Mum was never around either because of work. I don't mind being on my own. Anyway, the point is, the house is empty. It's the perfect place to meet."

I share a glance with Kieron.

"If you're sure?"

She nods. "I'm sure. This is important."

"OK, then, if we're agreed, I can reply to Joanna now and ask her to meet us this afternoon at your address, Ivy," Kieron announces, typing into his phone.

"I suppose that means you're all heading back to London," Rex surmises, unable to keep the disappointment out of his tone.

"You could come, too," Dad says brightly.

"Someone needs to stay here with the animals – my animals, I mean," he emphasizes, still holding a snoring Chomp in his outstretched hand. "Although I will miss these five! I'll also miss having a full house; it's much too big a space for one person. It's been wonderful having you here, thank you so much."

"Thank you for everything you've done for us," I reply.

"I'm going to spend the rest of the time we have here cooking up dishes for your freezer," Nan insists, jumping into gear and rushing over to the fridge to pull out a load of ingredients. "I'll leave you instructions on how to serve them."

"We'll keep you updated about Joanna," Kieron assures him.

"Thank you." Rex smiles gratefully. "Yesterday I started writing up a piece about Luna's innocence, drawing on all the facts without pointing the finger at anyone else. Until we're certain who's involved, there's no point in stoking the fire, but at least we can start an attempt to clear Luna's name. I'll finish that and send it out to my contacts – maybe there's a paper that will run it. Your mum owns most of the big ones, Ivy, but no harm in trying to reach smaller communities through local news."

"That's a great idea," Lucy says. "Why don't we get a date in the diary for you to come visit the rescue centre, Rex?"

"I would love that," he gushes, his eyes lighting up with excitement. "In fact, I think there might be enough space here for another rescue dog or two, wouldn't you say?"

Silver barks, rushing over to him and jumping up

to try to lick his face, which encourages Rex's two dogs to do the same.

"I think that's a yes," I say, as Rex bursts out laughing, holding his hand up out of the way so as not to wake the snoozing gecko contentedly curled up in his palm.

Ivy's house is incredible.

Kieron's jaw practically hits the floor when we pull up to it. Hidden at the end of a curved driveway that's accessed by posh electronic gates, it's huge and modern with sharp angles and a glass exterior. It's so striking, the sight of it stuns us all into silence and we sit in the

car gaping at it for a moment, trying to get our heads round the idea that Ivy lives in a place as cool as this. I wish Nan was here to see it, but she'd insisted on going home once we returned to London – she was worried about what the paparazzi might have done to her lawn and she didn't want to skip another of her bell-ringing classes today. She's already missed the last two.

"Ivy, you live in a spaceship!" Kieron gasps as he jumps out the car.

"I think that's what Dad wanted people to think." Ivy chuckles.

"Did he design this house himself?" Lucy asks, closing the car door behind her and staring up at the building in awe.

Ivy looks embarrassed at our amazed reactions. "No, I think it was a famous architect who drew up the plans," she says quietly. "But I can't remember his name."

"Well, it's fabulous!" Lucy exclaims, smiling at her. "Very glamorous. It looks like it should feature on a TV show!"

"Actually, I think it did when it was first built," she admits, leading us across the gravel drive to the front door. "When my mum moved out, I think she was more upset to leave behind the house than me and Dad."

"I'm sure that's not true," Lucy says gently.

"She lives in one that has a similar design now," Ivy adds.

"It must be so cool to live in a place like this," Kieron muses, gazing round at the perfectly manicured lawns and the unusual steel water feature in the middle of the drive.

"You'd think…" Ivy sighs.

Dad and Lucy share a look, while Ivy reaches up to the control pad to the side of the door and punches in a code. A light on the pad goes green and we hear the clunking sound of the door unlocking. She pushes open the door and stands aside to let us traipse in. The whole ground floor is just a vast open space with modern art statues dotted around on pedestals and a staircase made up of wooden steps and glass panels on the far right of the room. The view from the back of the house is of their extensive landscaped garden that boasts even more art. But the most eye-catching feature when you first step in is the indoor waterfall straight ahead of you along the back wall.

"Whoa," I say, keeping hold of my ferret as he struggles to get free. "Blizzard is going to love splashing around in that."

Ivy chuckles. "When I look at it, it just makes me need to pee."

"I was just thinking that!" Dad exclaims.

"You can let Blizzard have the run of the place," Ivy says, noticing me grappling with him as he twists around in my grip.

"I don't know; everything is so clean and perfect. He might knock some very expensive art over or something."

"Don't worry, it's all fixed down *very* solidly so there's no chance of any of it being handled or broken. My parents made sure that nothing could be ruined by a child growing up here." She gives me an encouraging smile. "Seriously, the animals can go exploring."

At her permission, I set Blizzard down on the ground and he instantly pelts towards the waterfall, running slap bang into the glass that surrounds it. He shakes his little head in confusion and then, with a growl at the glass, attempts another go at getting to the water, headbutting the shield once again. Stripes stalks over to the stairs, going straight up to find a comfortable bed. Talon flits across to perch on what looks like a strange brass sculpture, but I assume is a very expensive work of art, and Chomp stays put on my shoulder, happy to do a tour with the rest of us.

Silver remains at my side, watching Blizzard with a bemused expression.

"Ivy, your house looks like the set of a James Bond film," Kieron remarks, impressed.

"It could definitely pass as the house of a Bond *villain*," she emphasizes, glancing up at the ceiling. "Mum would have loved that description."

"I think it's amazing," I say enthusiastically.

"It's flashy and big, but when you're on your own, it's cold and empty," she explains with a hint of sadness, before collecting herself. "Do you want to come up to the kitchen? We have a machine that makes coffee, tea, hot chocolate, whatever you like."

Following her up the steps to the state-of-the-art kitchen that sprawls across the second floor, we continue on a tour of the house and, once Kieron has finished gushing over the cinema room on the third floor and the swimming pool on the roof, we return to the kitchen and Lucy, Ivy and I take our places on the stools around the island while Dad and Kieron have fun pressing all the buttons on the drinks machine.

Kieron has just discovered the well-stocked cookie cupboard with resounding glee when there's a buzzing sound.

"That's the gate," Ivy tells me, rushing over to a keypad built into the wall of the kitchen, a screen above it displaying a CCTV view of the gate at the end of the drive.

A small red car is waiting to be let in.

"That must be Joanna," Ivy announces, turning to me. "Are you ready?"

"Ready." I nod. "Let her in."

Pressing a button, Ivy opens the gates and the car crawls up the drive to the house. I rush down the steps with Silver at my heels, heading outside to greet her. I nervously wait as she parks, desperate to ask her about Magnitude but also hundreds of questions about working with Mum.

The car door swings open and she climbs out. She's tall and young – in her late twenties, maybe – with a blonde pixie hairstyle, dangly earrings and rectangular black-rimmed glasses. She's wearing a thin purple scarf round her neck and a blue coat over a pink-and-green floral dress, with black tights and a pair of yellow shoes that have little bows on them. As she closes the car door behind her, it makes a creaking sound, which prompts her to roll her eyes and mutter to herself, "Must get that fixed."

Spotting me, the corners of her mouth lift into

a smile and she removes her glasses to reveal bright blue eyes.

"Luna Wolf," she says excitedly, coming over. She stops in front of me and looks me up and down. "I would recognize you anywhere."

"I have been on the front pages a lot recently," I concede.

"No, not from that. I'd know you because you look just like your mother." She exhales and smiles at me. "I can't believe I'm meeting Athena Wolf's daughter. What an honour. I owe so much to your mum … you have no idea. I'm really pleased your friend got in touch – thank you for inviting me here."

We may have just met, but I like her already. She's got a warm, friendly aura. I can understand why Mum saw her as a trusted protégé.

"Thanks for coming, Dr Slade."

"Joanna, please," she insists.

I beam at her. "Would you like to come in?"

As I lead her through the house and up the

stairs to the kitchen, she remarks on the fascinating architecture of the building and mumbles something about wishing her own house could be this clean. She introduces herself to everyone, paying particular attention to Dad – when he shakes her hand, she places her other one on top of his.

"Athena meant the world to me," she says quietly. "I'm so sorry we lost her."

"Thank you," Dad replies, and I can see that he's as convinced as I am that she was on Mum's side.

She gratefully accepts Lucy's offer of a drink, requesting a glass of water, and then she notices Silver, who decided to stay hovering around Kieron and the cookies as I went to get the door. She gasps and places a hand over her heart.

"It's him," she says, her eyes filling up. "I can't believe it."

She approaches him slowly and then crouches down, before holding out her hand to him, letting him come to her in his own time. Silver sniffs at her hand warily and I notice a spark of recognition in his eyes. With a small whine, he moves towards her and bows his head, letting her stroke his ears.

"Hello, you," she says softly. "It's been a long time. We never got to say goodbye, but I'm glad we've found each other again."

"We wanted to ask you some questions about Magnitude," Kieron says, watching her.

Joanna straightens, glancing around us anxiously.

"This conversation isn't being recorded, is it?" she asks. "I'm happy to answer your questions if you want the truth – I owe it to Athena – but I am quite senior at a successful company and if what I tell you gets out there and becomes twisted somehow so that my reputation is on the line, that could put the company at risk and ruin a lot of people's livelihoods."

"All we want is the truth so we can help stop these recent attacks and find out who has the other super animals," I tell her firmly. "We're not interested in selling any stories. You can trust us."

"I could always trust Athena," she says. "So I suppose I can trust her daughter. I'm not sure I can

241

be much help, I was so junior back then, I was a nobody…"

She trails off and takes a moment to steel herself, taking a sip of water and placing the glass down slowly on the counter. She looks up at Kieron.

"What do you want to know?"

Kieron looks to me for permission to launch into his questions and I give him a nod. He clears his throat and consults his notes.

"First, can you confirm for us that you worked at Magnitude with Dr Athena Wolf?"

She looks pained as she nods. "Yes. I'm ashamed to say that I did. Like Athena, I had no idea about what was really going on." She gives Silver a sympathetic glance. "They kept a lot of us in the dark. I wish Athena had told me when she discovered the truth. I felt so stupid when it all came out. I wish… I wish she'd told me so I could have helped her save the animals. She and I were close. I've never understood why she didn't let me help her – it's always troubled me. I would have done anything for her."

"I imagine she wanted to protect you," Dad says, lifting his chin. "She didn't want to involve anyone else and get them into trouble."

Joanna sniffs and pushes her glasses up. "Yes, that sounds like her. She was that type of person. She took all the responsibility and none of the credit. Athena took me under her wing. You have to understand, I was very shy and junior. She shouldn't have paid the least bit of attention to me, but she guided me in my career, encouraged me when I needed a confidence boost." She turns to me, her eyes shining. "I was her protégé."

"What about Dr Callahan? Did you work with him, too?" Kieron asks.

Joanna's expression darkens. "I worked with him, but I was not part of his team. Nor would I ever want to be. He was nice to my face, but I knew he was secretly horrible about me – your mum had my back, though, Luna. Athena was the only person who believed in me and because of her, I learned to believe in myself."

"And now you're high up in your company," Ivy says, smiling at her.

"Exactly. I was so unsure back when I worked with Athena, and very lost," Joanna admits. "I felt so much pressure because of my family and who I was. I didn't know who I could trust. Athena made me feel like I could be more than just my name, that I could be whoever I wanted to be. It really is thanks to her that I'm where I am today."

Kieron and I share a confused glance.

"Sorry, Joanna," he begins, "but, if you don't mind me asking, who are your family? What do you mean 'more than' your name?"

She's thrown by his question, scanning our faces and realizing that we're equally as puzzled by her comment.

"You… You don't know?" She runs a hand through her hair. "Oh dear. I thought that's why you wanted to talk to me today."

"We've been looking for a 'Joanna' who worked with Athena and I tracked you down through one of your articles," Kieron explains, before hesitating and adding, "Why? What should we know?"

"That I'm the daughter of the founder of Magnitude," she says slowly, clearly nervous about our reactions. "Hunter Gild."

CHAPTER THIRTEEN

Dad shudders at the name. Lucy gasps.

"Your dad is Hunter Gild," Kieron repeats in shock, before slapping his head with his palm. "How did I not realize that when I knew your surname? Of course, it makes sense that someone like him would be behind Magnitude."

"Hang on, how do you know her dad?" I ask Kieron, holding up my hands. "Should I know who Hunter Gild is?"

Joanna blushes. "You might have heard of him."

"He's one of the most successful businessmen

and entrepreneurs in the country," Dad explains. "He's well known for his … uh … persistent methods."

"Swap out 'persistent' for 'ruthless'," Joanna says, shooting my dad a grateful smile. "Thank you, though, for trying to be nice about it. I'm well aware of the type of person my father is. Conniving, brutal, cutthroat, controlling – take your pick. He will do whatever it takes to get what he wants and won't let anyone get in his way. He'll stop at nothing."

"He's an intimidating man," Lucy says tactfully.

Joanna raises her eyebrows. "He's terrifying. I know it's an awful thing to say about your father, but I've always been frightened of him."

"He came for dinner once when I was little and my parents were still together," Ivy recalls, leaning forward on the kitchen island. "I remember overhearing the fight my parents had after he left. I think Dad was worried about his influence over Mum. She thought he was an extremely savvy businessman and told Dad to mind his business."

"Savvy is an interesting way of putting it." Joanna sighs. "I suppose he is – but his shrewdness gets the better of him. He'd throw the most loyal of his friends under the bus to secure a good deal. How do your parents know him, Ivy?"

"My mum is Sarah Slade."

"Ah." Joanna nods. "Then you too must understand how it feels to grow up knowing that everyone is scared of your parent because they know how powerful they are and what they're capable of doing."

"Your dad is also known for his passion for collecting rare things, isn't he?" Kieron checks, typing Hunter Gild's name into the search engine on his phone.

"It's an all-consuming obsession," she emphasizes. "Like I said, once he's decided he wants something, he won't let anything stop him from getting it. Our family home was like a museum, filled with priceless artefacts from all over the world."

"Joanna," I say, treading carefully, "do you talk to your dad a lot?"

She balks at the suggestion. "Let's just say, we don't see eye to eye. I can't remember the last time we spoke. He sends me a Christmas card every year, or rather, his PA does."

"So you wouldn't know if he's started Magnitude up again," Kieron says, getting straight to the point.

She blinks at him. "You think… You think those new super animals that have been running riot around London are his doing?"

"We have no idea. You know your father and we don't," I point out hurriedly. "We appreciate you might not know, but do you think it could be likely?"

Joanna's eyes drop to the floor.

"I'd be lying if I told you the thought didn't cross my mind when I saw it on the news," she admits quietly. "Part of me hoped you really were the culprit, Luna, so I could safely know it wasn't him. But now that I've met you, I know that it's ludicrous to think you have anything to do with it. You're very much your mother's daughter."

She sighs, pressing her fingers to her lips as she

considers this line of thinking, the rest of us waiting patiently for her conclusion.

"I think there's a strong chance my father is involved," she says eventually, her face almost crumpling at the thought, but she manages to hold it together. "He… He always said he'd relaunch Magnitude. How could he *do this*?"

"We don't know for sure that it's him," Lucy reminds her. "This could all be conjecture and coincidence. It could be someone random who has come across the magic."

"Maybe," Joanna says, disheartened. "I should have confronted him before now. As soon as I saw those new super animals, I should have contacted him and … and stood up to him. I'm sorry, Luna. I feel like I've let your mum down all over again."

"You can't blame yourself," Dad says, as I nod in agreement. "If Hunter Gild is behind this then he's not an easy man to stop. I'm not sure there's much you could have done without evidence against him to bring to the police."

"He's good at covering his tracks," she says, her forehead furrowed in concentration. "The things he's got away with… I don't even want to think about it."

Lifting her glasses off her face, she rests them on top of her head and rubs her eyes, as though suddenly exhausted.

"The new super animals don't seem to want to work with their human in the same way that Luna's do," Ivy points out. "They seem out of control. Do you think there could be a glitch with the magic this time round that scientists would need to work on?"

"I have no idea. Athena was the only one who could wield the magic before, but this could be a different type," Joanna says thoughtfully.

"If your dad is behind this, might he approach you to help him fix the problems? You were one of the original scientists to work on Magnitude," Ivy says.

"That would require him having to speak to me *and* admitting he needs my help. He won't be doing either, trust me," Joanna informs her.

"If he does get in touch, do you think you could tell us?" I ask hopefully.

"Of course," she emphasizes, before giving me a grave look. "You're not thinking of going after my dad, are you?"

"We'd need evidence he was involved first."

"He's a dangerous man, Luna. You have to be very careful," Joanna says pleadingly to me. "If he even found out that I'd been talking to you" – she grimaces – "it wouldn't go well for either of us."

"Don't worry, she won't do anything silly … right, Luna?" Dad says with heavy emphasis, staring me down until I nod.

"I know it's been hard for you with the press pointing the finger in your direction. I'm so sorry I can't be of much help," she says glumly, before she notices the time on the clock on the wall and starts. "I have to go, I'm afraid, I'm late for a meeting. I'm sorry I didn't have the answers you were looking for."

"Thanks to you we know who founded Magnitude," I say. "We've been looking for your dad for a long time. Now we have confirmation that it's him."

"I suppose that's something then," she says, smiling at me. She glances at Ivy. "What does your mum think about you two hanging out? I get the feeling from the headlines that Sarah Slade isn't Luna's most supportive fan. Does she know that she's blasting your friend?"

Ivy shakes her head. "I haven't told her that we're friends. She wouldn't listen to me if I fought Luna's case anyway. There's no point."

"If you want my advice, you should talk to her about it," Joanna encourages. "Sometimes I wonder if things would have been different if I'd had the courage to talk to Dad about my friendship with Athena. Maybe if he knew how much she'd done for me, he might have had the respect to listen to her when it came to the animals."

Ivy tilts her head in surprise. "You really think I should ask my mum to stop the bad press about Luna?"

"I think it's worth a try. She might just listen." Joanna crouches down to say goodbye to Silver. "I hope I'll see you soon, old friend. Watching him transform into a wolf is so magical and there's nothing like seeing him run across an open space – I suppose he doesn't get to stretch his legs much here in the city."

"Just on rescue missions," I say, feeling a pang of guilt. "I wish there was a place we could go that was big and spacious and secret, where all the animals could just run free."

Joanna straightens and places a comforting hand on my shoulder.

"They *chose* you, Luna. They're happy with you," she says, and I thank her.

After a panicked moment where she thinks she's lost her glasses but then realizes they're on her head, Joanna says her goodbyes, promising us she'll be in touch if she finds out anything about her dad and assuring Kieron that he can email her if we have any more questions. After she's left, we gather around the kitchen island, listening to her car rumble back down the drive and through the gates.

Dad lets out a low whistle, shaking his head.

"Poor thing, growing up with such an overbearing bully of a father," he says. "She couldn't be more different to him! So sweet and bumbling – no wonder Athena was desperate to help her."

"Do you think Hunter Gild is the person we're after, Luna?" Ivy asks eagerly.

"I do. We just need to prove it," I state, feeling a surge of determination now we have a name. "Let's hope he makes a mistake."

I owe Dr Joanna Gild big time.

After a couple of days of thinking about it, Ivy decided to follow Joanna's advice and call her mum. She was convinced nothing would come of it, but she was wrong. Since their chat, the paparazzi have kept their distance and, although my name hasn't completely vanished from the news, it's not popping up on everyone's phone as a breaking news notification every five minutes or emblazoned across the top of every paper on the newsstand. It helps that there haven't been any recent public incidents involving the other super animals, although my worst critics have attempted to use that as evidence of my guilt.

"Luna Wolf spends her half-term break away from London and during that time, the city has no threats from wild animals. You do the maths," mused tabloid journalist Christopher Cricket, who recently appeared on a morning show to offer his opinion.

But the anger towards me in the media has definitely lessened in general and I know that I have Ivy to thank for that, *and* Joanna for putting the idea into her head.

Sarah Slade's newspapers have noticeably shifted focus away from me, finally leading with other national news stories. One article this week even suggested some alternative suspects for the tiara robbery. Nan has been in a much better mood now that the paparazzi aren't buzzing about her lawn, although she was cross to discover Constable Croft attempting to be undercover, watching the house through a pair of binoculars in an unmarked car parked across the street. The

press may have lost a bit of interest, but clearly I'm still under suspicion. Nan marched right over to him brandishing her frying pan to "have a little word". We haven't seen Constable Croft anywhere near the house since.

Joanna reaches out to help me further when she messages to say she's had a brainwave about a space where my animals could freely transform without being seen and have a good run. We arrange to drive in convoy one weekend with her leading the way to the place she has in mind.

"Where do you think we're going?" Dad asks, driving behind her car, which is so old and banged up, it's making strange sounds and has caused Nan to comment several times from the front seat that she's not sure Joanna's going to make it very far at this rate.

"No idea," I say, in the back with Kieron and Ivy.

Stripes is curled up in Ivy's lap, while Talon is perched on Nan's knee and Kieron is letting Chomp play on the window ledge on his side. I'm holding Blizzard steady as he perches on his hind legs on my lap, leaning on the ledge, looking out the window and squeaking at the other cars going by. Because of his size, Silver has to go in the boot, but he's leaning over so his head rests by my shoulder, his whiskers tickling my cheek.

"How mysterious!" Nan exclaims, before swivelling round to face us. "Speaking of mysterious, when were you three going to mention the school funfair?"

"What funfair?" Dad asks, frowning as he catches my eye in the rear-view mirror.

"How did you find out about the funfair, Nan?"

"Gerard has a granddaughter in your year and in our recent aerial yoga class he was telling me all about the big funfair that's being held in the school field next weekend!" she explains. "I told him you hadn't said a word to me about any such thing. Clearly you haven't mentioned it to your dad, either. Why would you keep it secret?"

"We weren't hiding it from you," I say, shrugging. "We're just not going."

I've done everything possible to keep a low profile at school since coming back from the half-term holiday: I've barely spoken in class, I insist on eating lunch in the library, which is the opposite side of the building to the canteen, and as soon as the last school bell of the day rings, I go straight home or to the rescue centre, missing all the extra-curricular activities and clubs. After the drama of The Pumpkin Party, I know that some of the parents were worried about me being at school with their children, so I've made sure that other students know I don't want to cause any trouble or make them feel uncomfortable. I'm doing my best to become invisible.

I'd forgotten about the funfair that the school is

hosting to try to raise money for the music and drama department. Everyone is excited about it and it's all anyone can talk about, but I've already accepted that I shouldn't go.

"You're not still insisting on hiding away?" Nan checks, raising an eyebrow at me.

"It's for the best, Nan."

"You should go to that funfair with your head held high to prove to everyone that you don't care what they think. You know you're innocent and that's all that matters. The paparazzi have backed off now. You deserve some fun!"

"I've told Kieron and Ivy that they should go, but I don't mind missing out."

"We're not going if you're not going," Kieron declares, before adding wistfully, "even if there's candy floss machines."

Nan eyeballs Ivy, but she shrugs, unfazed. "Who wants to go to a funfair anyway?" She smiles, nudging me with her elbow.

I can tell that Nan is torn about whether or not to

attempt to persuade us. She gives up and turns back to face the front, dropping the subject. She's a social butterfly and has always encouraged me out of my shell, but recent events have ushered me right back under it. Until Hunter Gild is caught, I'm not taking any chances.

After about half an hour of driving out of London, Joanna indicates to make a turn that would be very easy to miss – it's not signposted and the hedges surrounding it are overgrown. We drive down a long winding lane that gets narrower and narrower until it suddenly opens out on to what looks like a huge car park that was abandoned before it was finished, with only a few spaces marked out and the rest just a big square of concrete.

Beyond it is a large glass dome.

"Welcome to the Gild Botanical Gardens," Joanna announces, once we've climbed out the cars and stood in front of some old turnstiles to marvel at the building.

Passing through the creaky turnstiles towards the

glasshouse that's filled with plants and flowers, Ivy looks as though she's in heaven.

"What *is* this place?" she asks, bewildered.

"One of my dad's projects that he got bored of," Joanna explains. "He bought the land on a whim, got a famous architect to work with botanists to design the dome and then invested in some amazing rare and diverse plant collections. It was going to be a big tourist attraction, but by the time it was half-finished, Dad was distracted by Magnitude and gave up on it." She looks downcast as she adds, "I wanted him to let me take over. I still make sure that the plants are looked after properly."

"Are you sure we're allowed to be here, Joanna? It seems deserted," Nan comments.

"That's because it is," Joanna answers. "Dad never comes here. Technically, I suppose, he wouldn't be happy with our presence, but it's not like he'll ever know. The botanists I hire to care for the plants have told me that they've never met Dad. It's as though he's forgotten about it altogether. I haven't visited for ages, but I used to come here quite a lot. It's important to have a space where you can feel peaceful."

Joanna guides us through the glasshouse, quickly cottoning on that she doesn't need to give us much of a tour thanks to Ivy's encyclopaedic knowledge about nature.

"This is a shrub from Mauritius!" Ivy exclaims at one point, looking excitedly for Chomp, who is perched on my shoulder. "They're pollinated by geckos."

We watch in great anticipation for Chomp's reaction as he peers down at the plant. Sticking out his tongue, he blows a raspberry.

"He doesn't seem all that bothered," Nan observes.

"I guess he feels more like a crocodile than a gecko today," I say.

"That is one funny-looking cactus," Kieron comments, passing a row of them that are round, like green, spiky globes.

"It's officially called the *Parodia magnifica*," Ivy says. "But it is sometimes referred to as the balloon cactus or green ball cactus."

"I didn't realize you knew so much about plants, Ivy." Dad smiles at her expression of wonder as she admires her surroundings.

"To be the best environmental lawyer I can be, I have to know about what I'm fighting for," she answers. "How will I get a court to care about protecting nature if I don't know anything about it?"

"Very true," Joanna says, looking impressed.

"Why are there steps on that side of the dome leading up to the ceiling?" Kieron asks curiously, pointing at the metal staircase that curves round one side of the glass and seemingly leads to mid-air. "There are no other floors."

"The designer built that in so if Dad ever wanted to include really tall trees, someone would be able to reach the top of them."

We continue to admire all the plants and colourful flowers as we wander through to the other side, where Joanna leads us out into a garden that's been sectioned off with a fence. As soon as she steps outside, Joanna looks puzzled.

"What's wrong?" Dad asks.

Her forehead creased in confusion; she gestures to the space in front of us. "This… This is new. I've never seen this fence before. Someone has put this up recently."

"But I thought you said no one comes here," Kieron points out.

"They don't," she insists, aghast. "It's been abandoned for a long time. Dad didn't sell it, but he's never shown any interest in returning to the project. It's only thanks to me that most of these plants have survived. I don't remember any kind of planning permission for this fencing. Why would anyone section off this bit of land? It's so … *random*."

"It looks like that bit of grass within the fence has been trampled," Dad notices. "Does anyone keep livestock nearby?"

Joanna looks baffled at the suggestion. "Not for miles! This is private property. No one would have the guts to use my father's land without his permission, surely. And anyway, why would anyone want to bring their animals into this specific fenced-off space when they have all the land surrounding it for them to roam?"

An answer to her question begins to dawn on me.

"What if they weren't interested in letting the animals roam the land? What if they were more interested in caging them?" I suggest urgently.

Silver lets out an anguished whine, mirroring my feelings.

"If Hunter has been keeping those animals here, then he could come here at any minute," Kieron croaks. "We need to go now!"

Joanna clasps a hand to her mouth in disbelief.

"Come on!" Ivy says, waving us inside the greenhouse.

But as we enter through the back, we hear someone bark, "Who's there?", his voice echoing around the dome.

I recognize it immediately and my blood runs cold.

"It's Callahan," Joanna hisses, as we all stop dead in our tracks. "*Hide!*"

CHAPTER FOURTEEN

"Well, well, well," Callahan begins, a smirk creeping across his face. "Dr Joanna Gild."

Peering through the leaves, I see Joanna jut her chin out defiantly.

Silver and Stripes are crouched low next to me, and Blizzard and Chomp are safely tucked away on my shoulders. Talon has landed nearby on one of the branches, hidden from sight. Dad, Nan, Ivy and Kieron are behind us, ducking behind another huge leafy plant.

Callahan is here with – surprise, surprise – Dean and Chad.

"D-Dr Callahan," Joanna says, doing a bad job of hiding the wobble in her voice that gives away her nerves. "What are you doing here?"

"We could ask you the same question," Chad says gruffly, coming forward to look her up and down suspiciously.

"Yeah, we could ask you the same question," Dean repeats.

Callahan rolls his eyes.

"I look after the plants," Joanna answers. "I assume you're not here to do the same."

"No, I hate plants," Dean informs her. "We're picking up a piece of equipment."

"It's strange that you're here to care for the plants, Joanna," Callahan says calmly. "Your father is under the impression that you hire people to do that for you. I have the rota of staff that come here to do that."

"Every now and then I like to come here to check they're doing a good job."

Callahan remains unconvinced. "And the car outside?"

"It's mine."

"There are two."

Joanna falters. "I… I just bought the other one. I asked the seller to drop the new car off here."

"Really." Callahan looks bemused. "You were planning on driving that car home and leaving your old one here?"

"That's right," she says.

Callahan sniggers, before addressing the others: "Search the place."

Dean turns to do so, but Chad holds out his arm, stopping him.

"You seem to be forgetting that you're not the boss of us any more, Callahan," he grumbles in a low voice. "You don't get to tell us what to do."

"Oh yeah!" Dean exclaims cheerfully. "We can do what we like!"

Closing his eyes in exasperation, Callahan rubs his temples. "But wouldn't you like to find out who else she's hiding in here?" he seethes.

"If you want to search the place, why don't *you* do

it?" Chad poses stubbornly.

"Yeah, you're not too high and mighty to look around a few plants," Dean adds.

Dad reaches out to tap me on the shoulder and silently gesture for me to follow him. While they stand in the central path, their bickering offers us the perfect opportunity to sneak around the side of the dome to the exit. Ducking under stray branches and slowly and quietly pushing aside flowers and leaves, we gradually creep round in single file as Talon carefully flits through the plants, keeping an eye out to make sure we're not noticed.

"It makes more sense for you two to carry out the search," Callahan is insisting.

Chad snorts indignantly. "Why?"

"Because you're better at tasks that require muscle," Callahan reasons.

"Thanks! I do exercise when I can," Dean gushes.

"That makes you more adept at action-based requirements, while I'm more suited to the intellectual side of things," Callahan says in a sickly-sweet voice.

"He's playing mind games on us, Dean!" Chad insists angrily. "I'm not walking through a load of spiky plants and thorns while you stand here doing nothing, Callahan. You search the place and we'll stay here and talk to Joanna."

Callahan groans. "Argh, we're wasting time!"

"*You're* wasting time," Chad huffs.

"Go look!" Callahan orders.

"*You* go look," Chad retorts.

"What would we even be looking for?" Dean asks.

"FOR GOODNESS SAKE!" I hear Callahan bellow as we file out the door.

Once we're safely out of the building, I stop the others heading to the car, pointing out that if Callahan comes out and finds one of the cars gone, he'll know Joanna was lying and she could get in trouble. Instead, we hide behind the Information kiosk and nervously wait. After a while, the four of them emerge – Callahan is leading the way, followed by Joanna, with Chad and Dean bringing up the rear.

"I told you there was no one else here," Joanna is saying innocently.

"Fine," Callahan snaps, clearly irritated when he sees both the cars still parked next to his van. "Next time you buy a car, arrange for it to be dropped off at your house and not on your dad's property."

Joanna stops in her tracks, causing Chad to halt suddenly behind her and Dean to slam straight into his back. Ivy's shoulders shake with silent laughter and Kieron presses his hand over his mouth to stop him from sniggering.

"Watch it," Chad growls at his companion.

"I demand to know what's going on here," Joanna announces bravely, but I can see her hands are shaking.

Callahan rounds on her. "You don't have the right to demand anything."

"Why is there an animal pen in the grounds? Is it for the new super animals?" she asks boldly.

"We don't know what you're talking about," Chad says, feigning innocence.

"And if we did, then we wouldn't tell you anything about the super animals and the fact that we've relaunched Magnitude," Dean adds.

"So you *have* relaunched Magnitude!" Joanna says, her jaw dropping.

"*Dean*," Chad hisses. "What have I told you about thinking before you speak? You really are the most—"

"I want in," Joanna announces.

Callahan looks surprised. I glance at Kieron and he shrugs, as baffled as I am.

"I want in on Magnitude," Joanna repeats confidently. "I was one of the original scientists on the project and if my dad has relaunched it, then I deserve a spot on the team."

Callahan strokes his chin thoughtfully.

"From what I remember, you were Athena Wolf's biggest fan," he points out. "You were always following her about, desperate for her approval. When you found out the true purpose of Magnitude after Athena robbed us of our glory, you weren't best pleased."

"I was young and naïve," Joanna explains.

"So you're telling me that, say Magnitude *was* back up and running and we were able to produce more super animals, you would be interested in helping?" Callahan checks.

"That's right." She nods. "Didn't you think I'd work out that it was my dad orchestrating the chaos the new super animals have caused? I could have gone to the police and told them what I knew about Magnitude. Dad would have easily become the main suspect. But I didn't do that. Instead, I kept quiet because I know now that I want to help him expand his collection of these rare creatures. Think how powerful that would make our family. I want to be a part of that."

He nods. "I can see why."

"I've worked hard in my career and done well, but I want more than that. I want" – she searches for the correct word – "uh … power. And status. Please, Callahan. At least pass my request on to my dad."

Callahan inhales deeply.

"All right. I'll tell him you want to join again. It would be handy to have more *brains* on the team," he says pointedly, his eyes flickering to Chad and Dean, who both scowl at him. "If he agrees, then I'll tell you when to meet here. We can see if you remember any of the work from seven years ago."

"I remember it all," she assures him.

"Good. I'll be in touch," he says, before turning on his heel and heading to the van.

"Yeah, we'll be in touch," Dean echoes, scurrying after the other two.

"You don't need to repeat everything we say, Dean," Chad scolds, as they open the van door and jump up into the seats. "You sound like an idiot."

"*You* sound like an idiot," Dean snaps back, blushing.

"See? Repeating again. You need to start having original thoughts," Chad sneers.

"I have original thoughts! They're just too clever to share with you," Dean claims grumpily.

The van starts up and we hear them still arguing

as they drive away. We wait a good amount of time before we dare to come out of our hiding place. Joanna is standing exactly where she was when they left her. As we approach her, she exhales and her shoulders drop, as though she's been holding her breath this entire time.

"I know it was a bit of a spontaneous plan, but I figured that if they bring me on to Magnitude, we'll be able to catch them red-handed," Joanna says, biting her lip. "What do you think? Is it a good idea?"

"*I* think you're even braver than I thought," I tell her, a smile spreading across my face as she beams at me. "It's a great idea."

Nan keeps telling me off for always being home. She thinks I should be out more, spending time with my friends, joining after-school clubs or helping at the rescue centre with Lucy. Instead, she's constantly moaning about how much I'm "skulking" about the house, as she puts it. As I've told her, I need to be on hand in case Joanna calls to let us know that she's heard anything from Callahan. But it's been almost a week and he still hasn't contacted her. I've been checking in with her every day and she's promised that as soon as she hears, we will.

We're so close to catching Hunter and shutting down Magnitude once and for all.

"I've been thinking about this weekend," Nan tells me one afternoon when I've just got back from school. "We should go to the funfair."

I look up at her from where I'm sprawled out on the floor of the hallway, having been knocked down by Silver as he greeted me by jumping up and attacking me with welcome-home licks the moment I got through the door.

"Did you hear what I said, Luna, or am I talking to myself? I think that it would be good for all of us if we—" She stops mid-sentence as she glances at the table that sits in the hall with a vase of flowers on it and does a double take. Narrowing her eyes at it, she tuts, immediately going to open the cupboard under the stairs where she keeps a lot of her cleaning products. Nan often does this – she'll spot something that needs cleaning and won't be able to concentrate on anything else until it's spick and span.

"I was talking to Gerard earlier on the phone," she continues. "You know, my friend from aerial yoga. He was calling to ask if I would like to volunteer as a chaperone at the school funfair. He's on the committee and they've had someone drop out."

We hear the keys in the door behind me and Dad comes bumbling through, quickly shutting the door so as not to let too much cold air in. "Ah, hello everyone!" he says cheerily, shrugging off his coat and hanging it on a hook. "How was everyone's day?"

"Chomp came to school with me," I tell him, as he reaches out to ruffle my hair. "He napped through most of the lessons, but he found lunch break very entertaining."

Nan gives Chomp a disapproving look as he crawls out from my bag and scampers away down the hall, disappearing into the kitchen.

"I didn't realize he was in my bag," I add, noting her expression.

"All right, well, from now on, let's check our bags for geckos before we leave the house," Dad announces, fishing his phone from his pocket. He notices the cloth in Nan's hand and makes a face. "Ah, Clementine, if this is about the new stain in the sitting room, I—"

"What stain?" She gasps. "I was dusting the hall because of all the dog hair."

She glances down accusingly at Silver. Lowering his ears, he whines guiltily. She turns back to Dad.

"What stain are you talking about, Richard?"

Dad's cheeks flush and he pulls at the knot in his tie.

"Uh … nothing!" he squeaks. "Ignore me! No new stains anywhere!"

I try my best to stifle a laugh, while Nan darts into the sitting room to inspect every surface of the furniture and carpet. Dad quickly searches for something in his phone.

"I have exciting news," he announces, hoping to draw Nan back out of there. "With everything that's been going on lately, I put the house search on the back burner, but look at this. A house has just become available and it looks perfect for me and Luna. It's like fate! Clementine, come see."

While he waits hopefully for Nan to reappear, I check out the photos of the advert up on his screen.

"It looks amazing," I gush, examining the spacious rooms and huge garden. "Can we afford this, Dad? It looks much bigger than the other ones you were viewing."

"By some miracle, it's in our price range, and it's not too far, either!" he says enthusiastically, pointing to the pin on the map displayed below the photos. "This email popped up in my inbox today. I must have signed up for alerts from this estate agent. I signed up to so many different ones. I called straight away to book a viewing and they can fit us in to take a look on Saturday afternoon. Isn't that great?"

"Let me see," Nan says, too curious not to come

back to the hallway. She peers at the pictures over Dad's shoulder as he holds up the phone for her. "Oh yes, that looks very nice."

"Would you like to come to the viewing with us, too, Clementine?" Dad asks.

She hesitates. "Well, that depends."

"On what?" Dad asks.

She nods to me. "On Luna. I've been asked to chaperone at the school funfair on Saturday afternoon. The committee are looking for a volunteer. I would love to help them, but I'll only do it if Luna goes to the fair with her friends. Otherwise, chaperoning won't be quite so fun."

"Of course, the funfair!" Dad runs a hand through his hair, making it stick up untidily. "I completely forgot."

"It's no wonder you forgot. Luna has been refusing to go," Nan reminds him, crossing her arms and turning to me. "I think you should allow yourself a bit of fun. You can bring your phone with you and if Joanna calls, you'll still be able to pick up. Things are better at school now. So why not have a day off from thinking about Magnitude constantly? Or at least an hour or two?"

"I have to agree with Nan on this," Dad chimes in. "It's been a tough term. If anyone deserves to play some silly games and whizz round on a Waltzer, it's you, Luna."

Stroking Silver's head, I pretend to be thinking about it, but if I'm honest, I've had a change of heart when it comes to the funfair. It's been hard to listen to everyone at school talking about it excitedly, but the worst thing is seeing Kieron and Ivy pretend they don't care when it's obvious they do. They won't go if I don't, so there's only one thing for it.

"All right, I'll go to the funfair."

"Lovely!" Nan exclaims, clapping her hands. "I'll go put the kettle on for a cup of tea and then ring Gerard to let him know I can chaperone."

"I hope that's OK, Dad. I'm sorry I'll miss the house viewing."

He wraps an arm round me. "It's no problem,

Luna. I'm pleased you're going. You should enjoy your weekends! Lucy can come with me and if I like it, I can easily just book another viewing for you to see it. Your opinion is the one that matters most."

"Thanks, Dad," I say, resting my head against his chest. "I hope you do like it, but I'd also be sad to leave Nan."

He sighs. "Me too. She'll miss us, too, I'm sure."

We hear Nan suddenly give a yelp in the kitchen.

"Uh-oh. Gecko in the butter dish, do you think?" Dad whispers to me.

"Or gecko in the cutlery drawer?"

"WHY IS THE GECKO IN THE TEAPOT?" she shrieks.

"Whoops," I say, "I forgot to tell her he's taken to hiding in there!"

"On second thoughts," Dad comments with a snigger, as I burst into uncontrollable giggles, "I don't think Nan is going to miss us *that* much."

CHAPTER FIFTEEN

We arrive at the funfair to hear upbeat pop music blaring through the speakers set up around the field interspersed with the joyful screams from people being spun around on the rides and cheers from groups of friends gathered around those attempting to win prizes on the game stands. With the colourful flashing lights from the rides, the white festoon bulbs strung around the stalls, and the smell of hot chocolate and fresh crêpes filling the air, it feels like we're stepping into a small winter wonderland.

"They've really gone all out," Kieron remarks, looking about us impressed.

"Are you OK, Luna?" Ivy checks, noticing a group of students glancing our way as we walk in.

I'm prepared for the attention, though, because, as well as arriving with Nan, Ivy and Kieron, I also have Silver with me on the lead. The funfair posters state that well-behaved dogs are welcome to come and I wanted Silver there with me. No one has any reason to be scared of him, unless they're a secret evil villain. This way they can see that for themselves.

"I'm fine," I assure Ivy, admiring all the stalls and games. "Where should we start?"

"Marina Puddleton is coming over," Kieron says, as a girl in our class nervously makes her way towards us.

"Puddleton?" Nan repeats quietly, intrigued. "She must be Gerard's granddaughter."

"Hi, Luna," Marina begins, stopping in front of me and offering an apprehensive smile. "I'm really glad you came today. I wanted... I wanted to say I'm sorry for the way I acted before. We all are." She gestures at her group of friends keeping their distance but keenly watching our exchange. "I don't think you were ... um ... the reason those bad animals were let loose in London. Sorry that I didn't believe you."

"Oh! Thanks," I say, marvelling at the influence of social media.

Rex's column had spread quickly on several platforms and sparked a proper debate about the incidents and how quick the press had been to turn against me. I'd amassed a decent support group thanks to his fair and well-argued article. One of Sarah Slade's papers even ran his follow-up article that focused on the rescue missions we'd done with the emergency services, which made people even angrier that I'd been villainized when I'd been using my magic power for good.

Thanks to the increasingly positive image of me, I was made to feel much more welcome at school. My classmates started speaking to me again and I wasn't picked last for teams in PE (something I had got used to recently).

When I still insisted on eating in the library rather than the canteen, Kieron was confused, pointing out that I was a hero again. I explained that I was finding the yo-yoing between being a hero and a villain very tiring.

I'm not sure I want to be either.

Marina points at Silver. "Is that … your wolf?"

"This is Silver," I answer, tensing and putting a protective hand on his head.

"Would it be OK if I pet him?" she asks hopefully.

I smile, my shoulders relaxing. "Sure. He'd love that."

She crouches down to his level and holds out her hand for him to sniff. He licks her fingers, making her giggle and giving her the confidence to stroke his head. Proving how friendly he is, Marina then waves her other friends over.

"He's very gentle," Marina tells the others, scratching Silver's neck until he rolls over on to his back and accepts belly rubs from all of them. "He's a big softie! Is he really a wolf, too, Luna?"

"Of course he is, Marina," one of her friends answers. "Haven't you seen the video of him online when he transformed with the others to save Frederick Flair?"

"What about the video of when he saved that guy from the bridge in the woods?" another friend cries enthusiastically. "That was so cool."

"He's such a good boy," Marina emphasizes, tickling his chin until his tongue lolls out.

Nan leans over to whisper in my ear, "He's a hit. If only we'd known that all we had to do was to let you bring Silver into school to meet all your friends."

"Shall we go get some candy floss?" Kieron asks

impatiently, as more and more people crowd around Silver at the funfair.

"I think we should go on the rides," Ivy says, eyeing up the Waltzer. "What do you reckon, Clementine?"

"You won't see me on any rides, Ivy," Nan replies, looking sick at the thought. "You go off and enjoy yourselves, though, and I should report to Gerard. Have you heard from your dad, Luna?"

I check my phone and see I've got a message from him.

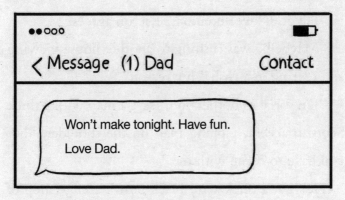

Won't make tonight. Have fun.
Love Dad.

Frowning, I peer at the message.

"Is everything all right?" Nan asks, noticing my expression.

"He says they can't come."

"That's a shame. But obviously they like the house if they've been there this long. They must be really taking it all in," Nan notes cheerfully.

"He hasn't mentioned the house in his message, which is weird." I hold up my phone so she can read it herself. "It's a bit strange, isn't it?"

"In what way?"

"He doesn't usually sign off his messages 'Love Dad', and he always puts some emojis in there, but in this one there are none."

"He does love an emoji," Kieron agrees.

"Maybe he was rushing to another house viewing and texting in a rush," Ivy reasons.

"I'm sorry to bother you," says a man with a thick Scottish accent, tapping Nan on the shoulder, "but you have to come with me."

He's got a thick wiry black beard, a huge mop of hair and such overbearing eyebrows that we can only just make out his dark beady eyes peering out from underneath them.

"Oh, are you coordinating the chaperones?" Nan asks enthusiastically.

He gives a sharp nod. "Sure."

"All right, lead the way." Nan hesitates, tilting her head at him. "Have we met before? I think I recognize you, but I can't think where. I know! Are you in the local amateur dramatic society? I went to see the recent production of Red Riding Hood!"

"Yes," he says, offering his arm to her. "That's it."

"Wonderful!" she exclaims, taking his arm as he leads her away.

"So," Kieron begins, clapping his hands, "should we maybe start with a sweet treat?"

Ivy rolls her eyes. "Come on then, let's go get some candy floss."

"Great idea!" Kieron says, marching over to the queue.

I tell the crowd surrounding Silver that we're going to have to go, prompting a chorus of disappointed groans and a grumpy snort from Silver, who was having a great time being so adored.

Waiting in the queue for candy floss, I'm in the middle of reassuring Silver that he'll have plenty of time to enjoy the company of his newfound fan club when I hear my name. I turn round to see Joanna darting through the crowds, looking around her frantically.

My heart leaps. I rush over to greet her.

"Joanna! What are you doing here? Have you heard something?"

"There you are, Luna, thank goodness you told me where you were going to be today," she says breathlessly, grabbing my arm. "I had to come find you straight away. They want me to go to the Botanical Gardens *now*."

I blink at her. "Now?"

"As in right this minute! I just got the message from Callahan and thought I should come get you on my way."

"Why wouldn't they give you more time?" Ivy asks, panicked, overhearing our conversation.

"To make sure I wasn't planning on springing

any surprises on them, I imagine," Joanna says drily. "They've done this on purpose. It's a test of my dedication. If I don't leave right this minute, they'll think I'm up to something."

"Then we can't waste another moment," I assure her, Silver barking in agreement next to me. "Let's go."

"We'll come with you," Ivy states.

"I'm sure Luna and I can handle this," Joanna says. "I would hate for all three of you to be put in potential danger. My dad might be there and who knows what—"

"We're a team," Kieron interrupts firmly, although he can't hide a wistful look back at the candy floss machine. "We're coming too."

"Has anyone seen Nan?" I ask, craning my neck to look over the crowds. "We need to tell her where we're going, she'll be worried if she can't find us."

"And what about your dad and Lucy?" Ivy points out. "They should come, too."

"We need to go *now*," Joanna presses, checking

her watch anxiously. "Can you message or call Clementine on the way and tell them to meet us there? Luna, if they think that I'm biding time to bring reinforcements or alert the police, they'll scarper and you can be sure that they won't leave one scrap of evidence behind. Our opportunity to rescue these precious animals will be gone. My father doesn't give second chances."

I bite my lip, knowing that she's right. I'm also aware that Nan will be furious at me when she finds out, but right now I don't have a choice. I hope she'll understand.

"We'll message them from the car. Let's go," I say, leading the way towards the exit.

"OK, great," Joanna says, tightening the belt around her long winter coat when it starts to fall loose. "I can't believe we're about to do this. I don't feel ready. What if Callahan brings a huge security team with him? How are we going to free those poor animals?"

"I know!" Kieron says excitedly. "Can we make

a stop? I need to pick up the tennis-ball blaster from the rescue centre."

"I have a much better idea. Let's swing by Nan's house," I say, glancing down at Silver, whose fierce golden eyes flash up at me. "If we're going on a rescue mission, we're going to need the rest of the team."

On the drive to the Gild Botanical Gardens, we start working out a plan.

"I wish you'd let me stop for the tennis-ball blaster," Kieron says, gazing out the window from the back seat as we speed down the road. "How are we going to take down Callahan and his men without it?"

"We have a giant wolf, a polar bear, a tiger, a crocodile and an eagle on our side," Ivy reminds him, pointing at Stripes, Chomp and Talon, who are settled on the seat between them, while Blizzard clambers on to her lap to try to get a good view out the window. "No offence, but I think they might be a little more useful than a tennis-ball blaster."

"Guess we'll never know," Kieron mutters under his breath.

"I don't think there's much point in me keeping up the pretence of wanting to be involved with Magnitude," Joanna muses. "They'll be able to see you all when we arrive, unless I drop you off before I drive into the car park and you find a way to sneak in once I'm inside? The risk would be them spotting you when you're still far off and having enough time to whisk the animals away before we have the chance to rescue them. I wouldn't be able to do it on my own."

"We need to get Luna and the super animals inside the dome before Callahan even knows what's going on," Ivy agrees. "That's a priority."

"Maybe I could simply run into the glasshouse with the animals. They take on Callahan and any other baddies, while I locate the three other super animals and bring them out to where you'll all be waiting safely by the car," I suggest, reaching to pet

Silver, who is hunched by my legs in the footwell of the front seat.

"That's a terrible plan," Kieron says bluntly. "You can't just run in there like you've done on other rescue missions. We're dealing with people who know how to handle super animals. They might have traps designed to bring down animals just like yours."

"Kieron's right," Joanna says, gripping the steering wheel so tightly her knuckles have gone white. "They'll be prepared. These people know how to deal with super animals. Did you notice the collars on the three animals they have?"

I gasp. "Yes! I remember seeing them flash red when we were dealing with them by the river after the tiara robbery."

Joanna swallows the lump in her throat, her eyes filling up.

"Callahan was always pushing for that type of thing years ago when Magnitude was first up and running. He thought it would be a good way to 'fire

297

up the animals', as he put it. Those collars jolt them into a panic, puts them on the attack. He thought it would be the best way to encourage their predatory nature and help others fear them."

"How horrible," Ivy whispers.

"Callahan is the *worst*," Kieron rages.

"I assume they're also designed to track them and that's how they've been confident letting them loose in London," she says thoughtfully. "Callahan's collar designs were always duds, but he must have been able to produce them this time round. No doubt my dad would have loved the idea of anything that helps him maintain maximum control. Your mum would never have allowed it, Luna."

"*Never*," I agree.

"She was able to control the animals without any type of collar." She takes her eyes off the road briefly to look at me quizzically. "How did she do it? How do *you* do it?"

"I can't explain it," I say, locking eyes with Silver as I try to find the right words. "It's not that I control the animals, it's more that we work together as a team. We have a connection that helps us understand each other."

"Through the magic?" Joanna prompts.

"I guess so." I shrug. "I honestly have no idea how it works."

"There *must* be a scientific explanation," Joanna says.

"You're not supposed to be able to explain magic," Kieron chimes in.

"We've got distracted. We still don't have a plan for when we arrive and we're almost there," Ivy points out as we approach the hidden turning. "If Luna isn't going to go barrelling in there with all the animals, what are we going to do instead?"

"Chad and Dean will be there, I'm guessing, and Callahan may have even gone all out and hired a big private security team," Joanna says, slowing the car. "The question is, how do we get past all of them to get to the animals?"

"They'll be able to see us as soon as we park. Slight

issue with a big glasshouse is that there's windows *everywhere*." Kieron sighs.

"So then there's not much point in a plan where we have to sneak in," Joanna says, looking deep in thought before she brightens. "What if we drew them out? We cause a distraction in the car park and Callahan and his men would come running out. Then, Luna, you sneak in and rescue the animals!"

"That's a great idea," Ivy says enthusiastically. "We draw them out to give you a chance of getting in there unnoticed. Do you think the animals are being kept in the glasshouse, Joanna?"

"Either in there or in that pen outside. I suppose it depends on what form they're in – they can't keep the elephant in the dome."

"What can we do to create a distraction?" Kieron ponders.

"It has to be big," Joanna says, as we creep down the narrow road getting closer and closer to the car park. She glances down at Silver. "Hang on – what if the animals were the distraction?"

"I suppose a polar bear plodding about would catch the eye," Kieron muses.

"You mean, I go into the glasshouse without the animals," I check.

Silver snorts indignantly.

"He won't let that happen," I translate for everyone else, before tapping my pendant. "Besides, I need to be there for them to transform. I need to touch them, remember?"

"But I'm not sure you should go in there with all the animals," Joanna says, looking worried. "If they overpower all of you at the same time, then the rest of us have no chance. It's risky enough you walking in there wearing your magical necklace."

"We could split up," Ivy suggests. "I'll come in with you and Silver, Luna."

"Kieron and I stay outside with the others and cause the distraction," Joanna adds. "That way, if things go wrong inside, you have us here to help."

"And if things go wrong outside, we'll be able to come help you." Ivy nods.

"But…" Joanna trails off, slowing the car right down so we're crawling along at a snail's pace.

"What?" Kieron asks. "I think that sounds like quite a smart idea."

"It's not that." She shakes her head glumly. "I'm not sure how good I feel about sending you in there, Luna. I'm the one who should take the risk. My dad is the reason we're here in the first place. He's the cause of so many bad things. I'll be staying outside while you go in and face it all. It doesn't seem fair."

"Joanna, you've done so much," I say sincerely. "Without you, those animals under his control wouldn't have a chance of anyone coming to rescue them. You are *not* your father."

She smiles, her eyes glistening behind her glasses.

"But you are so like your mother," she says kindly.

"I only hope I can be as brave as her when I walk in there," I say.

"You'll have me and Silver right alongside you," Ivy assures me.

"And we'll be waiting for you when you come

out," Kieron says. "Although we still need to come up with an idea to draw the bad guys out. What if Luna transformed one of the animals? It's enough to pique interest and leaves the others small and ordinary enough to go incognito for the time being until they're needed."

Joanna nods. "That could work."

"Maybe Stripes could transform," Ivy suggests. "Callahan's cronies wouldn't necessarily notice a lizard, ferret, or a bird. They can get to you quickly, too, Luna, if they need to transform. Talon can fly in and Blizzard could carry Chomp on his back and zip into the gardens to find you."

"OK, so here's the plan," I begin, mapping it out in my head. "Stripes causes a distraction in her tiger form, with Joanna and Kieron outside with her. Blizzard, Talon and Chomp remain in their small forms, staying hidden from the bad guys but ready to transform if anyone gets into trouble. In the meantime, I sneak into the glasshouse with Ivy and Silver, looking for the animals. When we come across Callahan, who will probably be guarding the animals, I transform Silver and we rescue them. Does that sound good?"

Everyone nods. The narrow road opens on to the car park and the glass dome looms ahead of us, a beacon of light in a vast open landscape of darkness.

"Once you've transformed Stripes, don't go through the turnstiles; they creak," Joanna reminds me. "Try going over or under them. Then hide behind the information kiosk and sneak in when the entrance is clear."

"Got it. We've got this, right?"

"Right," Kieron and Ivy chorus.

Joanna parks and turns off the engine. She turns to me. "Are you ready?" she asks, her brow furrowed.

Silver growls determinedly, filling me with the courage I'm looking for.

"We're ready," I answer.

CHAPTER SIXTEEN

At my signal, we climb out. Talon, Chomp and Blizzard take their position, hiding beneath the car, while Joanna and Kieron crouch behind it with Stripes. Ivy dashes towards the turnstiles, crawling under one, while Silver leaps over it with ease. They duck down next to the information kiosk and give me the thumbs up.

Stripes meows, brushing against my leg.

"You really are the best cat in the world," I tell her, crouching down and placing my hand on her back. She purrs loudly.

Doing my best to ignore the nervous butterflies

flitting around in my stomach, I close my eyes and focus on the magic of the blue pendant. I can feel it grow hot as the magic begins to flow from it, and with a flash of light, I open my eyes to find myself with my hand on the back of a majestic tiger.

Her golden eyes blink at me.

Stripes, you have my permission to cause a scene, I tell her.

She lets out a satisfied growl.

She waits until I've made my way to the kiosk and am crouched down next to Ivy. Then, with her ears pushed back and her chin raised, she emits such a loud, threatening roar that I wonder if the glass dome will shatter.

Ivy shudders next to me.

"I know it's Stripes over there," she whispers, watching the tiger in awe, "but she really is intimidating

when she's in her tiger form."

"Look!" I say, glancing to the door of the glasshouse. "It's working!"

Several security men have emerged, all of them armed with tranquillizer guns, but none looking particularly confident as they eye up the huge tiger prowling the ground ahead of them, her fangs on full display as she roars again.

"This one doesn't have a collar," a familiar voice says as a man passes the kiosk, oblivious to our presence. "Are we sure it's not just a wild tiger?"

"Wild tigers don't roam around England, Dean," I hear Chad snap back.

"How do you know there are no wild tigers in England?" Dean huffs.

"Because there *aren't*," Chad replies smarmily. "Anyway, she's definitely one of those super animals. Don't you remember that tiger from last time?"

"I remember the wolf practically chomping my leg off," Dean mutters.

Chad titters. "The wolf was in his ordinary dog

form when he nipped you."

"It was not a nip! It really hurt! He has the spirit of a wolf and jaws like one too," Dean hisses furiously. "My poor leg."

"Would you shut up about your stupid leg? I've heard nothing but you whingeing about your leg for months!" Chad complains.

"*You* shut up!" Dean retorts.

"Would you *both* shut up!" another man says furiously. "There is a TIGER over there and you two are too busy bickering to take care of it!"

Ivy nudges my arm and nods towards the door, which is now clear. Dean, Chad and their teammates have made their way past the kiosk and taken cover by the turnstiles. I don't move straight away, feeling sick with worry as they lift their tranquillizer guns and aim them towards Stripes. They take fire, but she dodges the darts with ease, before giving a ferocious roar, enraged by their shots.

We hear the men whimpering in fear.

"She'll be OK," Ivy insists, tugging on my sleeve. "We have to go now or we might miss our chance."

I know she's right. As I get ready to move, Stripes glances in our direction and catches my eye.

Be careful, I tell her.

Following Ivy, I hurry to the entrance of the glasshouse with Silver beside me and slip inside the door, ducking behind the first set of plants. We wait for a moment and when we can't hear anything, Ivy gestures for us to go round the edge of the dome, rather than down the path through the centre. Treading carefully around the plants, pushing leaves out of our faces and ducking under wayward stems and branches, I begin to wonder why we can't hear anything at all. No pacing footsteps or coughs from someone standing guard. No cat meowing, no mouse squeaking, no hedgehog snuffling.

Apart from us, it's still and silent.

We make it to the other side of the dome and look out the glass to the fenced pen outside, but it's empty.

"What do we do now?" Ivy whispers, looking as

confused as I feel.

"Let's go to the centre," I reply quietly, pointing to the middle of the dome. "There was a small clearing there with a bench, remember? He might be sitting there with the animals in their cages. But don't go down the path in case."

"OK. Be careful of the plants, some of these are very rare."

Finding our own way through the maze of plants towards the centre, we reach a pond and as Silver and I walk round it, I hear Ivy behind me gasp and say in an adoring, hushed tone, "*Victoria amazonica!*"

"What?" I ask, glancing at her over my shoulder.

"These are Amazonian giant waterlilies," she tells me excitedly, pointing at them floating serenely in the water. "They're the biggest of all waterlilies and really strong. They can grow up to three metres wide!"

We push on, ducking behind a big spiky plant that Ivy tells me is a blue agave.

"A large succulent grown on the west coast of

Mexico," she adds.

"Very cool," I say on autopilot, peering through the long leaves to see … nothing.

The middle of the dome is empty. Unless Callahan and the three animals are pressed against the glass somewhere along the opposite curve of the dome, which seems highly unlikely, there's no one else here.

"I don't understand," I say to Silver. "Where could they be?"

"Maybe Callahan isn't here yet," Ivy suggests, frowning. "Although, if that was the case, why would he want Joanna here so quickly?"

"Something's not right," I say, as panic begins to bubble through me. "I think he worked out Joanna was lying. We need to go back to the others before—"

Suddenly, the clear glass panels of the dome turn black, plunging us into darkness.

"Whoa, this must be smart glass," Ivy says, sounding a lot calmer than I feel as I fumble for my phone in my back pocket, unable to see a thing. "Handy for the plants that thrive in controlled light."

Before I can get my torch light on, a blown-up image of the front page of a newspaper is projected across the entire ceiling. There's a huge shot of my face as the lead picture below a headline that screams: "*BRITAIN IS SAFE AT LAST: Luna Wolf arrested and her eight animals detained*".

"What *is* this?" Ivy whispers, her head back and her eyes wide as she gazes upwards. She doesn't seem calm any more. She looks baffled.

Silver whines.

The picture changes to a different tabloid front page with another picture of me and the headline above reads: "*THE BIG, BAD WOLF: Luna guilty of city attacks!*"

"These are my mum's publications," Ivy observes warily.

As that image fades, another appears in its place with a similar headline, followed by another and then another, all of them claiming that I've been caught by the police and my out-of-control super animals have been safely locked up, so the nation is safe at last.

Ivy gasps at the final one, pointing to the top

right-hand corner of the picture.

"Luna, look at the date! These are tomorrow's newspapers!"

"How is that possible?" I ask breathlessly.

"Because we control your story," a familiar voice answers.

Cackling loudly, Callahan appears, stepping out into the middle, his hands clasped behind his back, a wicked grin across this face.

"Luna Wolf," he says, beckoning me to come out from behind the blue agave plant. "I hoped I'd see you again."

"I can't say the same about you, Callahan."

He chuckles at my reply and his eyes drop to Silver as we cautiously walk out into the clearing towards him.

"How sweet that you're still best of friends," Callahan drawls sarcastically, the smile fading from his face. "Shame you're about to be torn apart, but then again, you did steal the mutt from me in the first place."

"He was never yours to begin with," I say angrily, as Silver bares his teeth at him. "The magic chose my mum and then, when he ran away from you, Silver chose me."

Callahan sighs, looking bored. "You can twist the story however you like, Luna Wolf, but that fleabag belongs to Magnitude. You won't win this time. We're taking back what's rightfully ours."

Silver barks, making Callahan jump.

"These animals don't belong with Hunter Gild," Ivy says, narrowing her eyes at Callahan. "We won't let you take them!"

"Ah yes, Ivy Campbell–Slade. I've heard all about

314

you," Callahan says, looking her up and down. "You should pick your friends more wisely in the future. I'm afraid that your association with one of Britain's most notorious criminals is going to be very embarrassing for your poor mother. There's still time to switch allegiance, you know. Mr Gild will be happy to erase any reference to you in the articles if you choose now to help Magnitude in our fight to get back what is rightfully ours."

She balks at the suggestion. "I'd rather eat that Titan arum."

She points at a huge plant behind Callahan. He glances at it and then turns back wearing a confused expression.

"I'm sorry?" he says, his forehead creased.

"The Titan arum is one of the stinkiest plants on the planet. It's nicknamed the corpse flower because it smells like rotten flesh," she informs him.

The colour drains from Callahan's face. "Ugh. Suit yourself. Tomorrow, thanks to your mum, Ivy, your friend Luna and her reckless behaviour will be front page news," he informs us smugly. "Every media platform will be hailing those that brought you to justice and saved the masses from your wild super animals, who will be safely detained and placed in the care of responsible collectors."

"My mum won't do that," Ivy declares, her voice shaking.

"She's already agreed," Callahan grins. "Who else do you think mocked up these front pages for us? I think they look good. She certainly knows how to sell a story, doesn't she? Come tomorrow, you'll be the most detested person in the country, Luna."

"You'll never get away with this," I state.

One hand flying to my necklace, I reach towards Silver with the other.

"I wouldn't transform him if I were you!" Callahan says quickly, pointing down the pathway.

Ivy and I turn to see Kieron and Joanna being led in by Callahan's team. Blizzard, Chomp and Talon are locked in a cage that's wheeled in by Dean, who looks infuriatingly smug. Blizzard is throwing himself against the bars, while Talon flits around in there, knocking her head against the roof of it, and Chomp looks frozen in fear.

"Let them out!" I cry, instinctively lunging towards them, but Callahan stops me and pushes me back.

"Hand over the dog and the necklace," he growls, standing in my way.

"Never!"

"That wasn't a question, it was an order," Callahan says, gesturing at Chad, who is holding a tranquilliser gun against Kieron's shoulder, his other hand clapped round Kieron's mouth. Kieron is desperately trying to talk, his voice muffled.

"I think we shoot him anyway," Chad says, as Kieron attempts to wriggle free of his grip. "That would make things much easier."

"But we ran out of tranquilliser darts," Dean says, frowning.

There's a ripple of groans as the other men all turn to look in Dean's direction, shaking their heads at him. He realizes what he's revealed and grimaces.

"Whoops," he says quietly, hanging his head.

"You *numpty*!" Chad hisses, dropping the barrel of his tranquillizer gun down from Kieron's body, now that we know it's no longer a threat.

"We can take this lot if you transform Silver, Luna!" Ivy cries triumphantly. "They haven't got any tranquillizer left."

"Actually," Joanna says calmly, "we do still have this."

As she pulls a syringe full of yellow liquid from her pocket and holds it up next to Kieron's neck, my blood turns to ice.

I stare at her in shock.

"Oh dear, haven't you worked it out yet?" Joanna tuts, tilting her head. "I've been working for Magnitude all along."

CHAPTER
SEVENTEEN

"No," I whisper, desperately hoping this is some kind of mix-up. "*No*."

"To be honest, I thought you three would work it out sooner," Joanna sneers, while Callahan sniggers next to her. "But you didn't doubt me for a second."

Her voice and body language have changed so swiftly, I wonder whether I'm even looking at the same person. Gone are the apologetic, introverted posture, bumbling mannerisms and soft tone – she's taller, calmer, more confident. Her voice is projected and cutting, full of self-assurance. She takes off her coat and throws it on the bench to reveal a high-neck long-sleeve top, fitted leggings and heeled boots – all black, from head to toe. The opposite of the fun, bright, clashing colours we've seen her in before.

She gestures for one of the security team to bring to her the silver briefcase he's carrying. He holds it out for her while she unlocks it and lifts the lid, revealing the royal tiara sitting inside. She lifts it up and turns around to face me before carefully placing it on top of her head.

"It looks good on me, don't you think?" she says, raising her eyebrows at me.

Kieron wrenches his head free of Chad's grip. "We trusted you!" he cries, before addressing me. "The moment you, Ivy and Silver came inside here, she opened the car boot under the guise of needing something for the distraction, but it was that cage."

He nods to the contraption holding Blizzard, Chomp and Talon captive.

"She got the three of them in there before we realized what was going on," he adds, glaring at her.

"Yes, luring you all here and capturing your animals today really has been extraordinarily easy," Joanna declares, sniggering. "The best thing was that you've thought you've been in control of the situation all along. Didn't you question how easy it was to track me down in the first place? When you know how thorough Magnitude was to cover its tracks, did you honestly think we'd be so stupid as to let someone allude to the project and the leading scientist on it in a paper on stem cell theory?"

"You… You planted the story so I would find it," Kieron realizes, horrified. "That's why I'd never come across it before."

"I thought you'd need more time to trust me, but the first meeting at Ivy's house went so smoothly, I considered scrapping the next scene altogether and jumping to the end where we are now. However, I thought it was important for you to witness my run-in with Callahan, Chad and Dean, just to make sure you were fully convinced that I hadn't seen them in years," she says, relishing our shocked expressions.

"I think my and Chad's performances that day were particularly memorable," Dean opines proudly. "I've always thought I might have a calling in theatre."

"I believe it was me who had the lead role," Callahan says pompously. "I did most of the talking. All you two did was argue."

"Personally, I found your performance a bit boring," Chad tells Callahan.

"How *dare* you?" Callahan rages, puffing his chest out. "I'll have you know that—"

Joanna clears her throat pointedly. Callahan stops talking, but crosses his arms stubbornly, his face reddening with anger.

"You set us up," Ivy says, hardly daring to believe it.

"And you happily bounded into every trap we set," Joanna says breezily. "Getting Luna to The Pumpkin Party was a breeze. One simple fake radio communication and there you were at the scene of the crime, no questions asked. And today, you didn't hesitate to come running to the rescue. I didn't even have to worry about parents. All I had to do to keep your dad away was create a fake advertisement of his dream house and then ask one of my team to shut him and his girlfriend in a cupboard for the day. Your nan was a little harder to shake, though, wasn't she Dean?"

"She almost saw through my excellent bearded disguise," Dean reveals, before putting on a Scottish accent. "Aye, she was a tricky wee hostage!"

"Hostage? Where is she?" I croak.

"Left her tied up in one of the tents at the school fair," he says, back to his normal voice. "One of our friends is keeping an eye on her."

"How did you get here before us?" Ivy asks, confused.

"It wasn't exactly hard to overtake us in that pathetic excuse for a car I've been using," Joanna says, rolling her eyes. "I thought driving that terrible car around would be more convincing for the role I was playing. My collection of sports cars didn't really suit the character I was pretending to be. Thank goodness I don't have to put up with that red lump of metal out there any more."

"Hey!" Dean says, hurt. "When you asked to borrow my car, you said you liked it."

"Where's Stripes?" I ask, my voice wobbling as I think of Dad, Lucy and Nan.

"Oh, don't worry about your little tiger. She's having a nice snooze outside under the watch of some of my team," Joanna informs me with a sly smile. "She was very good at dodging the tranquillizer darts but didn't expect the shot I was able to give her when she was looking the other way. You see, Luna, my men were the real distraction. Not us."

"I don't understand," Ivy says. "How could you do this?"

"My mum thought you were a good person," I say, heat rising to my face in anger. "She thought you were the only person at Magnitude she could trust!"

"Your mum is the reason I'm here today!" Joanna shouts, momentarily losing her temper. She takes a deep breath and closes her eyes, collecting herself, before continuing in her calmer manner. I must have touched a nerve. "Athena Wolf was my mentor. She was the only person who believed in me."

"Now you repay her by doing this?" Kieron says, disgusted.

"What about what she did to me?" Joanna snaps. "I lost everything because of her! She and I had a vision: we were going to produce groundbreaking medicine produced from the magic Magnitude had discovered. I worked hard to prove myself to her, no one else. I looked up to her. What did she do? She stole the animals and destroyed my family's company without telling me a thing."

"She was protecting you! She didn't want you to be involved!" I argue.

"Athena would have known that Magnitude shutting down would affect me more than anyone else," Joanna says. "It was my father's project! Our family name's reputation. But she clearly didn't care. She didn't give me any warning. She left me behind to suffer the consequences of her betrayal. In the end, I guess she thought as little of me as everyone else did. So, I decided to prove everyone wrong and get the ultimate revenge on Athena Wolf: I would bring Magnitude back to its former glory."

"What about everything you told me about my mum helping you to believe in yourself? About how she guided you, how you wanted to do her proud and how I had her spirit. Was everything a lie?" I demand.

"Of course not, Luna. Without your mum helping me to see my full potential, I would never have had the confidence to help my father relaunch Magnitude," she replies smugly. "Hunter Gild founded the project, but it was me who kept the spark alive, and he'd admit that himself. Without me, Magnitude might have been buried when your mother first took off with those animals. When Callahan and those other scientists laughed at me behind my back, it was Athena who refused to let me quit."

Callahan shifts uncomfortably.

Joanna gestures to the ceiling, on to which a collage of images is now being projected, each one a different website or social media platform shouting about how much chaos I caused with my super animals and how lucky it is that I've now been stopped.

"Athena taught me that it was important to build and treasure connections with people as well as animals, and she was right. Dad had the contact, but it was me who made sure that Sarah Slade became one of our greatest allies – she respects me enough to allow me to control the future by pulling the strings of our national press," she explains, looking proudly at all the pictures displayed above. "Haven't you noticed, Luna? When I wanted you to be a villain, I made you a villain. And when I wanted you to be a hero, then a hero you became. You've surely noticed the change in public opinion towards you this week."

I think on how much better the last few days have been at school, how Marina and her friends suddenly think I'm wonderful again, and how the hatred in the press has all but disappeared. Watching my expression, Joanna's lips twitch into a triumphant smile.

"Yes, that was all me," she confirms. "I set up Ivy to make the call with her mum so the change in opinion wouldn't look too suspicious and Sarah was more than happy to go along with it all."

"She pretended to listen to me," Ivy whispers, her eyes filling with tears.

"Like me, your mum puts ambition and power before anything or anyone else," Joanna says proudly.

"In that case, both your lives must be empty," I say firmly, reaching over to take Ivy's hand and squeeze it.

"My life is anything but, Luna Wolf! Look what I can do!" she cries, letting out a chilling cackle. "With a few well-worded headlines and some powerful opinions from respected names in journalism, I can make you *whoever I want you to be*. Tomorrow, you'll be a villain again. This time, it will be your family who lose everything, and my family will be back on top – the heroes who have caught you red-handed and helped to protect the country from any further attacks."

"No one will believe you," Ivy says. "Everyone knows that the Gild family is only out for itself, trying to gain as much power and wealth as possible."

"They'll all believe me," Joanna replies, unfazed. "I'm the animal-loving scientist who has uncovered a terrible plot concocted by Luna Wolf to strike fear into the heart of the public and become as powerful as she can with a host of super animals on her side. When this story comes out, my father and I will be lauded and respected, and we'll have every single super animal in existence under our control."

"It's genius," Callahan says in awe.

"It's evil," Kieron corrects.

"In order to complete my plan, I am going to need that necklace of yours. I think it will go very nicely with my tiara," Joanna concludes, placing the tip of the syringe needle against Kieron's neck. "Hand it over, and let my men capture your dog, otherwise your friend here is going to get an injection."

"Don't do it, Luna," Kieron instructs firmly.

"Who knows what this much tranquillizer would do to a young boy?" Joanna muses aloud, examining the liquid. "It's strong. Just one drop would be enough to send him into a deep sleep. I'd hate to find out what happens if I give him the whole lot."

Silver barks fiercely at her, but she doesn't flinch. Instead, she pricks Kieron's skin with the needle, prompting Ivy to gasp, as I shout, "No! Don't!"

"The necklace, Luna," Joanna says sharply. "*Now.*"

I'm out of options. Silver snarls as one of the men nervously approaches him with a chain lead. The man stops in his tracks, his eyes widening with fear. If I reached out and touched Silver, I could turn him into a wolf, but the moment I do, Joanna could hurt Kieron. I desperately think of a way to rescue everyone, but I'm fresh out of ideas. I need time.

"NOW," Joanna barks, pushing the needle a touch further into Kieron's neck so he squeaks with pain.

"Wait, stop!" I cry, unable to watch.

Reaching to the back of my neck, I unclasp the necklace and hold it out. One of her security team takes it from me and passes it to Joanna. She cackles victoriously.

"Get that dog in the cage," she instructs her men.

"But you're holding the magic, he can't turn into a wolf without it," I plead, crouching down to wrap my arms around Silver. "There's no need to cage him."

"That dog can cause a lot of pain whether he's a wolf or not," Dean announces, causing Chad to roll his eyes and one of the other team to snigger.

"Shut up!" Joanna yells, glaring at Dean. "One of you get the dog!"

As someone throws the loop of the lead over Silver's neck, he barks, lunging at them and snapping his jaws in warning. The man who lassoed him squeals, jumping backwards and falling over his own feet in fright. Noticing Joanna's repulsed expression at his behaviour, he scrambles to his feet and holds the lead, watching Silver anxiously, beads of sweat forming on his forehead. Having got what she wanted, Joanna lowers her syringe and Kieron breathes a sigh of relief.

Easy, Silver, I tell him, as he growls and shakes his head uncomfortably, the chain tightening round his neck. *We're going to find a way out of this. I promise.*

The man gripping the lead gulps and points to the pool of saliva forming on the floor beneath Silver's jaws.

"W-why is he looking right at me and drooling so much?" he asks Callahan.

"Because he's eyeing up his dinner," Ivy mutters, causing him to whimper, his hands trembling even more than before.

Joanna lifts the necklace up to admire the pendant, whispering something repeatedly under her breath. At first, I can't quite make out what she's saying over and over, but then I hear her. "At last, it's all mine."

"Don't you mean it's all Hunter's?" I correct, hoping that if I can keep her talking and give myself a little more time, a new plan will pop into my head fully formed.

Lowering the necklace, but keeping it clasped tightly in her hand, she narrows her eyes at me suspiciously.

"Excuse me?"

"You're not in charge here, your dad is," I explain calmly. "He'll take that magic and the super animals, and you'll just be his puppet daughter doing all his dirty work for none of the reward."

"I am NOT his puppet!" she protests.

"I don't see him here today," I point out, feigning looking around the dome.

Her jaw clenches. "He's a very busy man."

"Because he's the CEO of Magnitude, while you're" – I pretend to think of the word I'm looking for before landing on it confidently – "nobody."

"I am NOT NOBODY!" she spits, her temper getting the better of her. "Not any more. Now, I am the leading scientist on this project."

"Yeah, but only because you're the boss's daughter." I shrug.

"That is not the reason!" she rages.

I notice Callahan purse his lips, giving away his opinion on the matter – he clearly agrees with me. Joanna spots it, too, and she rounds on him.

"You know I'm better than you, Callahan. You're just jealous! You weren't able to create more super animals, but I did."

"How?" I ask curiously.

"Ah!" Joanna begins, excited to tell the story. "Before she stole the animals and attempted to ruin our life's work, Athena was getting close to working out how to let others besides her wield the magic. She may have been chosen by the magical source, but if we were going to use the magic in animal care across the world, she knew it would be absurd for it to only work for one person. I was assisting her in her tests. When Magnitude shut down, I took her work before anyone could destroy it."

"I don't believe you," Kieron says boldly. "Athena would never leave such important work lying around. She was too careful. She wouldn't want it falling into the wrong hands."

Joanna rolls her eyes. "Fine, I stole it from her the day she took the animals. A stroke of luck that I got to it before she could take it with her."

"I bet she knew it was you," Ivy claims, jutting out her chin. "If she was on the fence about whether or not to let you in on her plan to rescue the animals, that must have made her mind up. She probably guessed that you'd nabbed any missing documents."

"So you finished the work my mum started, then," I surmise. "You figured out how others could use the magic. That still doesn't explain how you produced more super animals when the magic has been with me the whole time."

"Where do you think we got that magic in the first place, Luna?" Joanna sighs. "It didn't simply drop into your mum's lap. I went back to the Blue Mountains and, after years of exhaustive searching,

I found more. Not much, but enough. Your mum taught me never to quit, and I'm glad I didn't."

I blink at her. "The Blue Mountains in Jamaica?"

"That's right," Callahan declares, having been acting fidgety and impatient at Joanna getting all the attention. "Your mum talked about following some big butterfly, which would lead us to the magic. What a load of rubbish. Athena was always talking nonsense like that. Who has time to look for a stupid big bug?"

"The Jamaican Swallowtail is hardly a stupid bug, Callahan," Joanna remarks, bristling at his interjection. "But you're correct, I didn't have time to track them down. I just hired a large team to scour the mountain range instead. It was a tough slog, but we did it. Once I'd collected more of the magical source, I was able to create this."

She pulls out the delicate gold chain round her neck and holds up the pendant swinging on it: a jagged blue stone, very similar to the one that belongs to me.

"Athena was right about me. I am an accomplished scientist in my own right. Using this magic, I finally created three more super animals," Joanna proclaims, clasping her pendant in her fingers. "We no longer have to rely on who the magic chooses; we are able to use it as we please. I have achieved what Athena couldn't!"

"It's not that Athena couldn't work out how to get others to wield the magic. She didn't *want* to risk someone like you being able to do it," Kieron tells her. "She was right to be wary and put a stop to it before it fell into the wrong hands."

"Besides, you failed in the end," I tell Joanna, who inhales sharply at the accusation. "Your animals are out of control when they're in their super form."

"That is a tiny hiccup that I'm working on," Joanna spits, her eyes flashing in anger. "We will fix it very soon, isn't that right, Callahan?"

"Oh… Uh … yes. Yes, absolutely." He nods. "In the meantime, we have the collars."

I cross my arms. "He doesn't sound too confident to me."

"No, he doesn't," Ivy adds.

Joanna seems rattled for a moment, but then collects herself.

"Enough chit-chat, I have to get these animals to their new home," she says, wiggling her fingers at the cage holding Blizzard, Chomp and Talon. Blizzard hisses at her. "Thank you for being so obliging, Luna. I'm afraid I will have to hand you over to the police with the evidence I've created that you were behind the unfortunate incidents. I also have to make sure Sarah Slade has all the information she needs to make those scandalous headlines pop. Tomorrow, you'll lose everything, just like I did when your mother stole from me."

"I can't believe I trusted you. You won't get away with this," I yell at her, panicking.

"I already have," she says, a sinister smile creeping across her face. She holds up my necklace, letting it dangle from her hand. "Magnitude finally has what is rightfully ours: the magic and the super animals, and no one is going to take that away from us. Not this time."

Suddenly, a cry of, "We'll see about that!" echoes around the dome.

Our heads all jolt up at the same time as we hear a whooshing sound from above.

A figure comes elegantly tumbling down from a long silk fabric attached to the very top of the staircase that stops at the ceiling of the dome. Taking Joanna completely by surprise, they kick the necklace out of her hand. It skitters along the floor to me and I swipe it up quickly, gripping the pendant tight in my hand, before glancing up again to see who has come to our rescue.

I should have known.

Nan.

CHAPTER EIGHTEEN

"Did you really think you could keep me from saving my granddaughter?" Nan cries, landing effortlessly. "Never underestimate a nan! Luna, are you all right?"

"Much better now you're here," I say, beaming at her.

"Clementine, watch out!" Ivy yells.

Nan spins round to see Joanna furiously retaliating by readying the syringe of tranquillizer. As Joanna lunges towards her, Nan hastily darts out of her reach and then unclips the small frying pan she has hanging from the waistband tied round the top of her yoga leggings. She swings it through the air and there's a loud clang and a howl of pain from Joanna as it makes contact with her hand, sending the syringe flying out of her clasp. It clatters on to the floor in front of me.

"One should never travel without their frying pan!" Nan declares gleefully.

Callahan and I make a move for the syringe at the same time, both throwing ourselves on the ground with our hands outstretched. He gets there just before me but drops it when Ivy leaps on top of him, flattening him against the floor.

He yelps, turning his head as he lies sprawled like a starfish, Ivy pinning him down with her elbows.

"I think you broke my nose!" he splutters.

Before it can find its way to anyone else, I chase the syringe as it skids away and then, with all my might, I lift my foot and stamp on it.

Cradling her sore hand, Joanna glances up at the loud cracking sound beneath my foot and sees the syringe shattered, the liquid oozing out.

Enraged, she lets out a shriek of frustration before turning to the man holding Silver's chain.

"Do NOT let that dog near Luna!" she shouts, using her good hand to remove the tiara and place it back in its case, shutting the lid firmly. She glances up at her team, who have been too shocked by Nan's surprise entrance to move. "What are you lot standing around for? Do something!"

They spring into action. A couple of them run to help keep Silver captive as he strains and pulls to get to me, snapping and barking, while the others pelt towards me.

"Run!" Kieron cries, as he sticks his leg out to trip up Dean, who's rushing past him.

There's a loud "Oof!" as Dean falls flat on his face, followed by Chad yelling, "You're an embarrassment, Dean! Don't just lie there taking a nap! Do something! You really are a useless—"

CLANG!

Chad is silenced as Nan knocks him over the head with her frying pan. He crumples to the floor, freeing Kieron, who makes a beeline for the animals' cage, but is slowed by Dean, who wraps his hands round one of Kieron's ankles.

"Luna, hide!" Ivy orders, jumping to her feet and leaving Callahan cupping his nose with his hands to go help Kieron as he grapples with Dean.

As I turn and dart into the safety of the plants, I hear Joanna shout, "Whatever you do, don't let her near the animals! She has the necklace. If she touches them, they can transform. Capture her, for goodness sake! It shouldn't be hard, she's a little girl!"

Stealing a glance through the leaves, I spot Nan swinging her pan around dangerously, causing Joanna to hastily back away from her.

"Will someone PLEASE STOP THIS NAN?!" Joanna roars, and one of her men comes to her aid, jumping in front of her wielding a baton. I catch a glimpse of the sparring match between frying pan and baton and see Joanna slip away out the back of the dome towards the fenced area outside. Hearing footsteps nearby, I duck, remaining hidden by keeping low to the ground as I forge a path through the plants.

I try to map my way round to Silver, who is busy keeping his handlers on their toes, in the hope that I can jump out and reach him before I'm apprehended. I can keep track of roughly where I am thanks to recognizing plants that Ivy named on our way through and eventually reach a spot I know to be roughly behind where Silver is being held.

I'm just about to jump out when someone behind me yells, "GOTCHA" and grabs me round my waist, throwing me off balance and sending both of us tumbling forwards into the clearing. Silver barks and tries to pull towards me, just inches away from my fingers, yelping as he's yanked back by the chain.

Face down on the floor, I try to wriggle free away from the man who knocked me forwards, but he's managed to roll on to his front in time to grab hold of both my legs.

"*Get off!*" I say, trying as hard as I can to clamber forwards, but barely moving an inch, his hold is too strong. He sniggers in response.

"A weakling like you is no match for someone as strong as me," he shouts.

Whoosh!

A spherical cactus the size of a melon soars overhead and lands right on top of his bottom. He gasps, his eyes wide as saucers, before screeching in pain and instantly letting go of me. I watch as his hands reach to the cactus, only for him to yelp again as its spikes sink into his palms and fingers.

"You may have strength, but Luna has one better: she has friends!" Ivy cries, as she carefully lifts another cactus ball from the row of them nearby. "Take *that!*"

She pelts it at one of the men helping to hold back Silver. It narrowly misses him as he jumps out the way, dropping the chain to shield his head with his arms. Seeing Ivy pick up another cactus, the others holding Silver abandon their task to take cover in the plants behind. No one is stopping him now.

As he rushes to my side, I don't hesitate, reaching out to place my palm on his back. I barely have to focus for the magic to work. It's instinctive. My necklace glows and a blinding flash of blue fills the glasshouse. The light fades to reveal a wolf where Silver stood just moments ago. He throws back his head and his howl echoes round the dome, sending shivers down my spine. I hear the fearful gasps of Joanna's men as they realize what they're up against. When Silver turns to me for instruction, I know that my eyes are the same striking golden as his.

Free the others, I communicate.

With a ferocious warning snarl, Silver leaps over to the cage, sending the braver few of Joanna's team, who'd considered protecting it, scarpering. With a swift swipe of his paw, he breaks the lock and the door swings open. Blizzard darts across the floor in a blur, scuttling up my leg, while Talon soars over carrying Chomp. They land on my shoulder and the glasshouse is once again encompassed in a shimmering blue light.

I get to my feet, flanked by a crocodile, who scuttles ahead of me snapping his jaws, an eagle, who lets out a high-pitched call as she swoops in a circle overhead, a polar bear, who pushes himself up on to his back legs to let out a bloodcurdling roar, and a wolf, baring his teeth and growling as he bows his head, preparing to pounce on anyone who dares come close. Ivy and Kieron come to stand with us, both of them holding a cactus ball. Nan, who has shown Joanna's security men that a baton is no match for an item of kitchenware if you know how to wield it, completes the gang by joining us, lifting her frying pan as though it's a baseball bat, ready to swing.

Still holding his nose, Callahan finally stands and looks up at us.

His eyes widen in fear.

He whispers something inaudible.

"What did you say?" one of the men calls out from behind a plant.

"I s–said … RUN!" Callahan bellows, turning on his heel and sprinting as fast as he can towards the exit, pushing others out the way.

Give them a bit of encouragement to leave quickly, I instruct the animals.

I know polar bears can't laugh, but I swear I hear Blizzard snigger.

All four of them chase after the men down the main path, causing a panicked uproar amongst any stragglers. There's a loud splash as Chomp crawls into the pond, the top of his slender snout gliding through the water, nudging away the ginormous lilies as he closes in on a couple of the men hiding on the other side. They glance up to see his jaws wide open and scream, scrabbling back through the plants as fast as they can.

Joining the crowd running away, Dean glances back over his shoulder at a snarling Silver and nervously cries, "Nice doggy!", before hurling himself through the door, leaving Chad lying in the middle of the clearing of the dome on his own, still groggy from the force of Nan's frying pan.

"They're getting away with it!" Ivy huffs.

"Oh no, they're not," Nan tells her, a smile spreading across her face as we see flashing red and blue lights beyond the turnstiles. "After I escaped from the tent, I made a call to Constable Croft on the way here. I told him that I'd forgive him for all that wasted time hanging around my house if he came to help us capture the real villains. He said he'd bring the whole force if necessary. I see he was true to his word."

"What about Joanna?" Kieron asks.

We hear the distinct stomp of an elephant coming from the fenced area outside.

"I'll deal with her," I declare. "Could you go check on Stripes?"

"Don't worry, we'll make sure she's OK," Kieron promises me. "You go save the day."

I turn to address my animals as they come back from their chase.

The animals out there are not the enemy, I tell them.

Silver gives a bow of his head in understanding.

"I'll be right behind you," Nan says, giving me a nod of encouragement.

With the super animals hot on my heels, I make my way to the back of the now eerily silent dome and outside into the crisp, cold air. I'm greeted by the piercing trumpeting sound of a distressed elephant and see him hurling himself around the ground. The cheetah darts around in a frenzy, clawing at the fencing as though trying to rip a hole through it. The rhinoceros is at the back, pawing at the ground, his head bowed low, his horn pointed in our direction. He grunts angrily.

Joanna is standing beyond them, behind the fence at the back.

"Give me your magic and those animals, Luna, or I'll set these three upon you all!" she bellows.

"They're not really under your control, are they," I point out, trying my best to sound calm as I reach the gate of the fence. "It's over, Joanna. Your team has deserted you."

"We don't need them!" she spits. "My father and I don't need anyone!"

"You needed my mum. It sounds like she needed you, too. She really did believe in you. There's still time to prove her right. Turn these animals back and we'll look after them."

She shakes her head. "No. No! I won't give up. That magic belongs to us. This fence won't hold for long" – she points at the elephant, who is throwing himself against it, causing the structure to creak under his weight – "or I can let them out this side. They will hunt you down unless you do as I say!"

"Joanna, please stop this," I plead. "I don't want any of these animals to get hurt."

"One last chance, Luna Wolf," she yells, holding the pendant of her necklace up so I can see it glowing. "Give me your magic or I will send these super animals to attack!"

"My mum knew that there would be terrible consequences if this magic ended up in the wrong hands. She risked everything to make sure that wouldn't happen."

Joanna is watching me, waiting in anticipation. I take a deep breath, steeling myself before continuing: "I'm willing to do the same. I won't let you take the magic or the animals."

Looking as though she might explode with anger, Joanna lets out a strangled cry and then yells, "ATTACK THEM!" at the top of her lungs, her pendant glowing stronger. She reaches forward and throws open the gate at the back of the fence, providing the animals with an exit into the open. She cowers out of the way.

The rhinoceros is the first to notice the opening, thundering towards it, closely followed by the swift cheetah, and then the elephant, who'd been the furthest from Joanna, stomping around at our end of the pen. My animals prepare to defend, Blizzard rushing to the front of our pack and lifting himself on to his hind legs to cover me with a mighty roar.

I don't know how, but suddenly I know exactly

what to do. It's as though I can hear Mum's voice guiding me somehow. Because of her, I feel calm and in control.

Stepping around Blizzard, I turn to face him and hold up my hand.

Stop, I say.

He instantly drops to all fours. Silver whines anxiously.

"Luna!" I hear Nan shout out somewhere behind my animals, sounding terrified.

I spin back to face the cheetah sprinting right at us, having overtaken the rhino. I can feel the magic of my necklace radiating through me more powerfully than ever before. It begins to shine so brightly that I can feel the heat of the pendant against my skin.

My eyes fix on the cheetah's as she thunders at me.

I'm not going to hurt you, I try to communicate. *You're safe with us.*

She skids to a stop barely a few metres away.

I promise you, it's going to be all right. You don't have to be scared, I tell her.

Something changes in her eyes.

The rhino and elephant begin to slow, too, coming to stand next to her.

We're not going to hurt you, I emphasize to all of them. *We're going to protect you.*

"What's happening?!" Joanna screeches in the distance. "Why is the light in my pendant dimming? What are you doing, you useless predators? Attack, I tell you! Attack!"

You're safe now, I assure the three of them, ignoring her and keeping all my focus on the animals in front of me, who are swathed in the glittering blue glow of my pendant.

To prove I'm being truthful, Silver lies down next to me, resting his chin on the ground. Blizzard follows his lead, plonking his bottom down with a thud. With his jaws firmly closed, Chomp lowers his head, and Talon comes to land next to him, tucking in her wings.

In a burst of light, all of them change back to their everyday forms. I stand in front of the cheetah,

rhino and elephant with my gecko, sparrow, ferret and dog. I'm defenceless.

Will you let me help you? I ask the three super animals.

As they slowly bow their heads one by one, I know they can hear me. There's another flash of light from my necklace and the cheetah, rhino and elephant have disappeared. In their place is a stunning, bewildered Bengal cat, a shivering hedgehog and a nervous little mouse.

We hear a roar of anger from the other end of the

pen. Joanna comes charging towards us, yelling at the animals as she gets closer.

"NO! I didn't tell you to change back. You don't make the decisions. I control you with this, remember?"

She lifts her pendant furiously, only to come to a halt and stare at it in shock.

"Why... Why has it changed colour?" she cries, shaking it vigorously. "It's gone grey. Why isn't it glowing blue?"

She shakes it again, but nothing happens. It no longer resembles the jagged piece of rock hanging round my neck, but an ordinary grey pebble.

"I don't understand," she croaks, aghast. "What's happened?"

"Don't you see? The magic doesn't control these animals," I tell her, gazing down at the creatures in amazement. "They make their own decisions."

"No, no, that's not right," Joanna protests desperately. "If we want them to transform, then the magic makes them do so! Any time Athena wanted them to become super animals, she used the magic. You do that, too!"

"Only when there's a good reason," I explain calmly. "These animals transform when they want to, like when someone is in trouble and needs their help. My mum was researching this magic for medical advancement, in the hope that it would make animals better, not so that humans could take control of what they do and who they are."

"That's why you were never really in control of these animals, Joanna," Nan says, stepping forwards and placing a hand on my shoulder. "The magic chose Luna to be the one to wield it, in the same way it chose Athena. But the animals chose her, too. Silver came looking for her." She gestures to the mouse, hedgehog and Bengal cat. "These three never chose you, Joanna. They've been fighting your authority all along."

"Animals can't choose who controls them," Joanna seethes, shaking her necklace one more time. "They belong to me. I command them to do something and they do it. That's how this should work."

As the Bengal cat moves to sit next to me and the hedgehog and mouse come scampering over too, Nan chuckles softly.

"They've chosen who the guardian of their magic should be," she asserts proudly. "That's why your necklace has lost its glow and Luna's shines brighter than ever before. You have no power any more, Joanna."

Joanna lowers the necklace slowly, letting Nan's words sink in as she accepts the truth. She lets the delicate chain slip through her fingers, dropping the pendant on the ground. Her eyes close in despair. We hear footsteps behind us and see Constable Croft approaching, handcuffs at the ready.

"It's over," Nan emphasizes.

There's a growing whirring sound overhead and we're hit by a blustering wind so forceful it almost sends Nan and me off balance. The hedgehog curls up frightened at my feet, spikes at the ready. A helicopter appears above us, dropping down within the fence, its door sliding open. Joanna smirks.

"It's not over, Luna Wolf," she cries above the noise. "We'll never give up until that magic is ours and the animals belong to us once again!"

With that, she turns on her heel and races across the grass to the helicopter, climbing in and slamming the door shut. I start running after her, Silver darting ahead, but it takes off as soon as she's in, hovering above us.

Although I can't make out the face of the person sitting opposite Joanna, I can see the light glinting off the chunky gold watch around his wrist.

The helicopter flies into the distance and all I can do is stand there helplessly, watching Joanna and Hunter Gild get away.

CHAPTER NINETEEN

Leaning back in his armchair, Rex Robinson removes his glasses and sighs.

"It's quite a story," he says, gesturing to the open laptop resting on his knees. "Not exactly the ending you hoped for. There's been no sign of Joanna Gild?"

"None," Ivy confirms. "The police have searched and searched, but she's vanished. They think she might be hiding abroad somewhere. Hunter is in the wind, too. The Gild family has a lot of contacts, they'll know someone who can keep them hidden away for the time being."

Rex nods, before glancing up at me. "I'm sorry, Luna."

"Don't be," I say cheerily with a shrug. "The most important thing is that we rescued the animals. We'll catch Joanna eventually, but for now at least, we've saved Swift, Lance and Tusk from a life of being stuck in a cage."

Swift, the Bengal cat, lifts her head to meow gratefully, curled up on a velvet cushion that Rex found for her – it belonged to Stripes when she lived here with Rex, but as she has so many, Rex felt she wouldn't mind lending Swift one of them. I did notice Stripes giving Rex an unimpressed look when he plumped the cushion up for Swift, but she chose not to protest in the end and went back to snoozing on her favourite armchair.

Lance, the hedgehog, and Tusk, the mouse, are outside running about in one of Rex's paddocks, playing happily with Blizzard. Talon is somewhere amongst the trees lining the fields and Chomp is down by the brook with Nan, who fancied a walk along the stream whilst taking a phone call – she didn't say who it was, but judging from her smile, I'd guess it was Gerard Puddleton. Silver is stretched out on his side along the rug by the fireplace, dozing contentedly.

When Rex invited us to come to his countryside manor in the aftermath of everything that happened at the Slade Botanical Gardens, Nan accepted the invitation with great enthusiasm. It turns out that while five super animals under one roof is a challenge, living with eight is near impossible. But I didn't want to separate the animals straight away after rescuing them, because I knew that Swift, Lance and Tusk felt safer amongst the company of my five.

Luckily, Rex has more than enough space and, as long as they don't upset his rescue donkeys and llamas too much, they're free to roam his land as they please. The rest of us are happy to have escaped London for a bit, too. Dad and Lucy are currently enjoying a long walk in the fresh air, something they're very much appreciated after being shut away in a cupboard for a few hours by one of Joanna's employees posing as an estate agent.

After Callahan was caught, he admitted to the police where our parents were being held hostage and Chief Superintendent Reece went to personally rescue them herself. They were fine … if a bit shaken. They'd been much more worried about us.

"I wish I'd been there when Joanna revealed her true colours," Dad had seethed when we filled him in on everything. "I would have given her a piece of my mind! She betrayed us and she betrayed Athena's memory. Athena really believed in her."

"But Joanna didn't win," Nan had told him in her most comforting voice. "The animals and the magic are safe. That's what matters."

He agreed, but I knew he was still really angry, so I told him about how I'd heard Mum's voice when Joanna set the super animals on me. I said that it felt as though Mum was still looking after all of us, even protecting Joanna from herself.

He looked much happier after that.

While I'm really looking forward to things getting back to normal – well, as normal as they can be – I'm happy that Chief Inspector Reece spoke to Ms Sanderson, our head teacher, and we were given permission to have a couple of days off school this week to recuperate.

Kieron didn't sleep a wink the night following Joanna's escape, choosing to stay up to write down everything that happened, worried he might forget an important detail if he didn't note it all right away. Like his account of our last run-in with those responsible for Magnitude, Kieron has written it up in the style of a long newspaper article, but he's said that he won't publish this one, either. He just wants to keep a record of our adventures.

"This is very good writing," Rex tells him, passing him back his laptop. "Thank you for giving me the privilege of reading it before anyone else."

Kieron blushes at the compliment.

"At least they arrested Callahan," Rex continues, reaching for his cup of tea on the table next to his chair. "I hope he stays in prison this time."

"Sergeant Croft is confident he won't get out early this time, and neither will Dean and Chad," Ivy informs him. "And the royal tiara has been returned safely, too. The experts will be checking it over and hopefully putting it back on display so the public will be able to enjoy it, too."

"I'm pleased to hear it." Rex raises his eyebrows. "Did you say *Sergeant* Croft? I thought he was a constable."

"He's been promoted due to his work on this case," Kieron says with a smile. "It was him who made all the arrests at the Gild Botanical Gardens. He says he owes it all to Clementine."

"You really do have the coolest nan in the whole world," Ivy says to me.

"So, what now, Luna?" Rex asks, clasping his hands across his chest. "Your name will be cleared; everyone will be on your side again. Are you going to go back to helping the police force on rescue missions? What was it they called you? Oh yes, the 'Super Amazing Animal Champions' or whatnot."

"The 'Super Animal Adventurers'," Kieron corrects, laughing.

"Chief Superintendent Reece did offer me my old job back," I admit, "but I told her that, for now, I wanted to focus on school. No more playing at being a hero or a villain. I'd really like to just be … me for a bit."

Rex smiles warmly at me. "That sounds like a sensible decision."

"Next term will be very busy, anyway," Ivy notes excitedly. "Kieron is going to launch his school newspaper and I've founded the school's first botanical club. First thing on the agenda is to lobby to save the Gild Botanical Gardens. I've found out that Hunter Gild has applied for planning permission to knock down the dome and build a block of luxury apartments on the site. We have a lot of work to do to save all those plants."

"That will keep you busy," Rex says, impressed.

"Yes, I'm excited to see the botanical club *grow*," Kieron emphasizes, before bursting out laughing. "You know! Because plants grow!"

"Very good." Ivy sighs, rolling her eyes. "Anyway, Clementine inspired me to start it. If she's passionate about something, she throws herself into it. Like aerial yoga or cooking or singing. I want to be more like her. I want to be more Nan."

"We *all* want to be more Nan," I agree, giggling.

"Have you spoken to your mum, Ivy?" Kieron asks carefully.

She shakes her head. "I'm not ready to speak to her yet after everything she's done. Anyway, she's much too busy working with her lawyers to prove her innocence after the police found all those mocked-up front pages tearing down Luna. She's saying she had nothing to do with it and Joanna made up their entire relationship."

"I'm really sorry, Ivy," I say, noting her downcast expression.

"Me too." She sighs, lifting her chin. "But it's OK. It's not like we really had much of a relationship before. And anyway, I've got you lot now."

"Exactly." I nod.

"Did she say you're launching a school newspaper, Kieron?" Rex asks.

Kieron puffs out his chest. "That's right. I can't understand why we don't have one already. I pitched it to Ms Sanderson and she gave it the go-ahead."

"I take it you're editor-in-chief?" Rex smiles.

"Yes. And I'm also the news editor, and the features editor, and the arts and culture editor, and the sports editor. Oh, and the photographer." Kieron exhales, looking mildly panicked. "I really need to hire some staff."

Rex chuckles. "It will be fantastic. Now, the first issue of any newspaper is always the most important one. It has to grab everyone's attention, which begs the question: what will be your lead story?"

"I haven't got one yet. But I'll make sure it's good."

"It has to be better than good," Rex insists. "This is your introduction to the world! This is your chance to show everyone who you are as a publication and what you're trying to say. You have to decide what your paper stands for, what it calls into question, and what it celebrates. So, Kieron, editor-in-chief, what does your newspaper stand for?"

Kieron gulps. "Uh… I—"

"The truth," I interject.

"That's right," Ivy agrees. "Kieron's publication will have as much integrity as he does. There won't be agendas or manipulation of the facts. It's a newspaper you can trust."

Kieron blinks bashfully at the floor, sliding his glasses up his nose.

"Sounds like the sort of publication I'd be interested in reading, then," Rex says. "You just have to find a lead story that makes that clear."

"I think I have an idea," I say, causing all of them to turn and look at me with great interest. "You should publish this one."

"This what?" Kieron asks, confused.

"This story. Our story. Magnitude, Hunter Gild, Joanna, the super animals, me, my mum – all of it," I outline. "You've already written it, so it shouldn't be too much work to prepare a front page."

He blinks at me. "Luna … are you sure?"

"Yes," I say firmly. "I'm sure. People know enough already. We should tell them the truth about it all – and there's no one else I'd trust more with it. We've already done one interview together; this will be like the sequel."

"Wow." He smiles at me. "Thanks."

"That is quite a lead story," Rex says. "If this doesn't grab people's attention, nothing will."

Later that afternoon, Rex and Nan find me perched on top of the gate leading to the paddock. Silver is sitting alert on the ground next to me, his ears twitching at the braying donkeys.

"What are you doing out here in the cold? It's almost dark!" Nan scolds, as Rex passes me a coat and, once I've pulled that on, Nan hands me a mug of steaming hot chocolate. "Here. Drink this. I thought you might come in for it."

"Thanks, Nan," I say, clasping the hot mug in my fingers that have gone numb from the cold. "I was going to call in the animals, but they're having too much fun to come inside. I gave up trying to persuade them."

They follow my eyeline to where Blizzard is darting through the grass with Tusk. We can't see Talon, but we can hear her tweeting in the distance.

"Where's Chomp?" Nan asks, pulling her coat around her tightly. "He's not still down on the rocks by the stream, is he?"

"There's lots to explore down there," I justify. "He's having a great time. Lance is with him, there was a nice hedgerow nearby that he's become particularly attached to."

"Ah, lovely," Nan says.

I hesitate. "I know they love me and everything, but … I've never seen the animals happier. They really love all the space here, don't they. It's like they can really be themselves. Look at Blizzard." We watch as he stands up on his hind legs and pounces on a plant. "A ferret with the spirit of a polar bear. I'm not sure he belongs in Tottenham with me. Or anywhere with anyone. Polar bears need more than a house."

Nan and Rex share a look.

"Luna," Nan begins gently, "are you saying you think you should … free the animals?"

I swallow the lump in my throat, before giving a sharp nod.

Deep down, I think I've known for a while that these super animals aren't your average pets and that it doesn't seem all that fair for them to be living with us in the city. My mum felt the need to hide them here with Rex because she knew the people at Magnitude would come looking. Now that so many people know of their existence, there will always be someone out there who may want to capture them for their own gain.

"It would be irresponsible of me to insist they stay

with us," I manage to blurt out, my voice wobbling. "They deserve to be in control of their own lives. They will be safer out there in the wild than with me. No one will be able to track them down. And as long as I have the magic, then we'll always be connected. Keeping them with me would be selfish." I blink back tears to quietly add, "I just don't want to say goodbye."

"But it wouldn't be goodbye, not really," Nan tells me, placing a hand on my knee. "As you say, your connection with these animals extends beyond proximity. If you ever need them, no matter where you are, they'll come find you."

"Exactly." I take a deep breath. "I think it's important that I give them the choice."

"Clementine and I have already talked about this," Rex admits.

I look at him in surprise. "You have?"

"I had a feeling that you were thinking along these lines," Nan declares.

How do nans *always* know?!

"Rex had a wonderful idea that you could set

them free here, if you like," Nan continues. "That way they know where they are, and they can always find their way back here if they need."

Rex shifts uncomfortably. "And you can absolutely say no to this, because if they should be with any human, then of course, it should be you, but … well, I've always been a cat person, as well as a dog person, and Stripes and Swift do seem to enjoy the best of both worlds that is on offer here: the great outdoors for daytime exploring and a cosy fireplace at night—"

"Not to mention the hundreds of velvet cushions and luxurious armchairs on which to lounge," Nan adds, with a hint of disapproval in her tone. "You spoil them."

"I suppose I do," Rex chuckles. "Anyway, the point is, I wanted to offer my home to both of them. It is a very big house and the more animals here the better, I'd say. I like the company and you can come visit them as often as you like."

"They do seem to like it here," I admit, smiling at him as my eyes fill with tears.

"It is perfect for a couple of spoilt cats," Nan says.

"A couple of spoilt *big* cats," I correct. "Plenty of space to run free and a nice, warm bed to come home to. It really is the best of both worlds. They'll be very happy here."

"I know that no cat really has an owner, and certainly not those two, but I assure you I will be their loyal servant," Rex promises, making me laugh. "They'll want for nothing."

"I believe you," I say. "Thanks."

He looks down at the dog sitting patiently in front of me. "And Silver? What about him?"

"I guess I'll ask him now," I say, my heart in my mouth as I hop down from the fence, hand Nan my mug of hot chocolate, and then crouch next to him. "Silver, you have the choice to—"

But I don't get the chance to finish my sentence because Silver jumps up at me, sending me completely off balance. As I land flat on my back, he pins me down with his two paws on my shoulders and starts licking me all over my face, so that I'm laughing so much I can hardly breathe.

"All right, all right, I get it!" I cry, as his big snout looms over me. "You and I will stick together."

He barks satisfactorily and moves off, so I can sit up. Rex reaches out to help pull me to my feet, and he and Nan laugh while I wipe the dirt off my coat.

"I thought that would be Silver's answer," Nan asserts, as Silver leans against my leg and I stroke his head. "He is your loyal companion. I can't imagine you two ever being apart."

"Me neither," I say, sighing with relief.

"I'm very proud of you, Luna," Nan says, moving to put her arm around my shoulders. "I know how much these animals mean to you."

We gaze out at the animals playing together in the grass, swathed in the soft orange glow of the sunset.

"Yeah, but their freedom means more," I say, smiling out at them as Nan holds me tight. "And if ever they need, I know they'll always be able to find their way back home."

EPILOGUE

I hate goodbyes.

This was never going to be easy, but now the day has come to release the animals into the wild it seems near impossible. I know that this is the right thing to do. My mum once had to say goodbye to keep them safe. Now it's my turn.

But I don't want to let go.

The animals and I have walked past the donkeys to the far side of the field, while Dad, Nan, Lucy, Kieron, Ivy and Rex wait for me at the gate. They've already had their tearful goodbyes and are here to support me as I wave the animals off for good. Last night I spoke to each animal individually, telling them how much they meant to me and how they'd changed my life. I told them I'll miss them every day. I hope they know that.

My heart won't stop aching.

"On you get," I instruct them softly, and they each come close.

Stripes meows until I pick her up and she lounges in my cradled arms. Chomp is on my right shoulder, Talon is perched on my left, and Blizzard is tucked round my neck. Tusk and Lance have scurried on to my shoes. Swift leans against one leg, her tail curling round it, and Silver leans on the other.

I close my eyes.

The field is awash with a glimmering blue light and I'm surrounded by a team I never thought I'd ever be lucky enough to be a part of, the family I had no idea I needed.

There's the rhinoceros, who I've discovered to be comically stubborn and sweet.

There's the elephant, who's clumsy and ditzy and full of joy.

The intelligent, independent, belly-rub-loving cheetah.

The wise, elegant tiger, who always makes a bad day better with her warm, affectionate cuddles.

The curious and cheeky crocodile, whose adventurous spirit never fails to make me smile.

The fun, mischievous polar bear, who makes me laugh until my cheeks hurt and my belly aches.

The regal golden eagle who watches over me and makes my heart soar when she somersaults through the air.

And there's the wolf, my loyal companion and best friend.

Surrounding me in a semicircle, they all look at me with sad, knowing eyes. A tear falls down my cheek.

It's time, I tell them.

Silver whines, hanging his head.

Thank you for everything you've given me, I say, scanning my eyes across them. *Be safe out there. If you ever need me, you know where I am.*

I can't say goodbye. They can't seem to either.

Instead, I offer them a watery smile and give them a nod.

That's their cue.

Lifting up her trunk, Tusk lets out a trumpet sound and slowly turns, wandering away across the open grass. Lance paws at the ground and then falls into a trot alongside Tusk. With a flick of her tail, Swift meanders off. Stripes looks me in the eye and gives a load roar before she bounds away. At least I know that I'll be getting big cat updates from Rex.

Blizzard comes over to me and bows his head, allowing me to place my hand on his muzzle. He closes his eyes briefly and then turns, plodding off in the direction of the river. Chomp snaps his jaws together a couple of times to make me laugh and then, satisfied he's leaving me smiling, he crawls off in the same direction as Blizzard. Talon, who has been perched on Blizzard's back, launches herself up in the air, spreads her wings and treats me to a display of somersaults before she soars away over the fields.

I hear footsteps approaching from behind. The

others have all walked over to stand alongside me to watch the animals go.

"You did it," Nan says, her eyes gleaming. "They're free."

Silver throws his head back and sends his friends off to their new life with a long, heartfelt howl that sends a shiver down my spine.

There's another flash of shimmering blue light and, as the animals transform back to the smaller versions of themselves, they disappear from sight across the field.

I glance down at the dog by my side and, as our eyes meet, I know that he's thinking the same thing. We may not know where the others are going, but one thing is for certain:

We will see each other again.

ACKNOWLEDGEMENTS

We are back! And I could not be more excited for the return of Luna Wolf! This action-packed book has been such a joy to create! With twists and turns and so much at stake, Luna is a girl on a mission to do right by these magical animals. I feel super proud of this body of work. The message is simple and powerful: be kind to animals, treat them with respect and admire their beauty. This adventure has reminded me of all the incredible animals I've been fortunate enough to encounter in my life, whether it be a rescue mission or in nature, or those I have loved and who have loved me in return. Animals can be there for us and show up for us in so many ways.

I'm so lucky to work with a passionate and dedicated team, so a huge thank you to the fabulous humans at Scholastic who have helped shape this wonderful book: Lauren Fortune, Aimee Stewart, Rachel Phillipps, Hannah Griffiths, Tierney Holm and Alice Pagin. Thanks also to my Bell Lomax Moreton family, Lauren Gardner and Paul Moreton, the brilliant Katy Birchall for her continuous hard work, and the very talented Deise Lino for her art.

Thank you to all my loved ones and every single person who has read one of my books. Thank you for taking the time to reach out and share your love for them. It means the world to me. I really hope you fall in love with this one too!

Love always,

Alesha X

Katy Birchall is the author of the side-splittingly funny *How Not To Be a Vampire Slayer* and *A Vampire Slayer's Survival Guide*, the *Morgan Charmley: Teen Witch* books, *The It Girl* series and the *Hotel Royale* series, *Secrets of a Teenage Heiress* and *Dramas of a Teenage Heiress*, and the *Find the Girl* YA series with YouTube stars Lucy and Lydia Connell. Katy was proud to be the author of a retelling of Jane Austen's *Emma* for the *Awesomely Austen* series, a collection of Austen's novels retold for younger readers, and the spin-off novel for the hit Netflix TV show, *Sex Education*. Katy also works as a freelance journalist and has written a non-fiction book, *How to be a Princess: Real-Life Fairy Tales for Modern Heroines*.

She has written three novels for adults, *The Secret Bridesmaid, The Wedding Season* and *The Last Word*.

Katy lives in London with her husband, daughter and rescue dog, Bono.

Turn over for a sneak peek

PROLOGUE

"Pearl? Pearl, wake up."

A hand gently nudges me and I bat it away grumpily, burying my face further into the squishy pillow.

"Pearl, it's time to get up," Mum sighs, shaking my shoulder a little more firmly this time. "Come on, rise and shine. It's seven a.m."

I groan as she stands and opens the curtains, letting a stream of bright sunlight into the room. Blinking hazily, I force myself to sit up and let out a loud, pointed yawn. My Cocker Spaniel, Rosy, who was sleeping soundly on the bed next to me, yawns in solidarity before bouncing over to give Mum a good-morning lick.

"You and I need to have words, Rosy," Mum tells her sternly, while giving her a scratch behind the ears. She turns to me, raising her eyebrows. "Have you seen the mess your dog has made?"

Her eyes flicker to the floor, and I crane my neck to have a look, bracing myself for whatever destruction Rosy has caused now. Rosy is my best friend in the whole wide world and, in my opinion, she's perfect.

I do have to admit, however, that she has a few . . . well . . . behavioural issues.

There was the time she ripped up the sofa cushions, covering the living room in foam and white fluff, and then she went on to chew through several important-looking wires, destroy the remote control and ruin my favourite backpack. Not to mention the many vases and photo frames she's smashed when she gets overexcited and zooms round the house in an uncontrollable whirlwind, knocking into tables and walls as she goes.

Mum still hasn't forgiven her for chewing her prized Manolo Blahnik red satin heels.

As I peer over the bed to see what trouble Rosy has landed me in this morning, I wince in preparation, hoping that it's nothing too bad, before letting out a sigh of relief when I see what Mum is going on about. My bedroom floor is littered with shredded toilet paper.

"That's fine!" I exclaim, slumping back on my pillow. "It's only a bit of loo roll."

"It is not fine," Mum emphasizes, as Rosy gets fed up of Mum's attention and jumps across the duvet to cover me in slobbery licks, her tail wagging happily. "You need to train her, Pearl. She's getting out of control."

Mum shakes her head at me as I tell Rosy what a good girl she is.

"So, how did you sleep?" she asks, picking some golden dog hairs off her smart black dress.

"Good, I think," I say with a yawn, rubbing sleep out of my eye. "How about you?"

"I didn't sleep a wink," Mum says, looking at me expectantly, the corners of her mouth twitching.

At first, I'm confused. Then it hits me.

I remember what day it is. Any sleepiness is gone in an instant as my brain kicks into gear. HOW HAVE I NOT ASKED HER THE QUESTION YET? I gasp, sitting bolt upright and leaning forwards to grab her hand.

"Are ... are the results in?" I whisper, my throat tightening with nerves and excitement.

Mum nods, taking my hand in hers and squeezing it. "Yes. The results are in."

"AND?" I squeak.

A smile spreads across my mum's face, her eyes twinkling.

"Pearl, we did it," she says softly, as though she can't quite believe the words coming out of her mouth. "You are officially looking at the new Prime Minister of the United Kingdom."